The Cambridge Manuals of Science and
Literature

THE EVOLUTION OF
NEW JAPAN

The Emperor Mutsu Hito

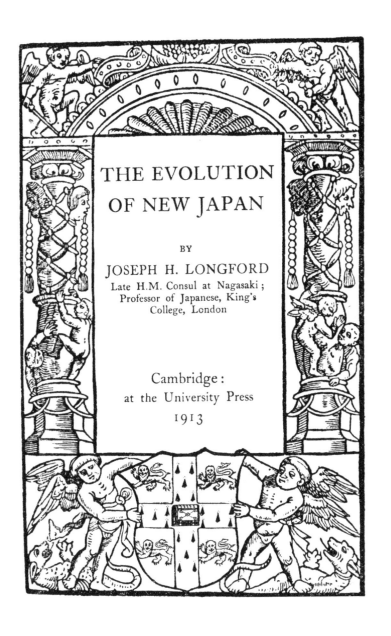

THE EVOLUTION
OF NEW JAPAN

BY

JOSEPH H. LONGFORD
Late H.M. Consul at Nagasaki;
Professor of Japanese, King's
College, London

Cambridge:
at the University Press
1913

CAMBRIDGE UNIVERSITY PRESS
Cambridge, New York, Melbourne, Madrid, Cape Town,
Singapore, São Paulo, Delhi, Tokyo, Mexico City

Cambridge University Press
The Edinburgh Building, Cambridge CB2 8RU, UK

Published in the United States of America by Cambridge University Press, New York

www.cambridge.org
Information on this title: www.cambridge.org/9781107697256

© Cambridge University Press 1913

First published 1913
First paperback edition 2011

A catalogue record for this publication is available from the British Library

ISBN 978-1-107-69725-6 Paperback

*With the exception of the coat of arms at
the foot, the design on the title page is a
reproduction of one used by the earliest known
Cambridge printer, John Siberch, 1521*

PREFACE

THIS little book has at least one original feature. It is, to the best of the author's knowledge, the first book on Japan which has ever been issued at the price of one shilling. Surely, this will commend it to readers and bookbuyers, even if it exposes no more than the skeleton of the modern history of a people who are both our allies and our good customers (as well as our rivals) in trade, and who can now give us valuable lessons of patriotic courage, sacrifice, and perseverance in return for all we have taught them.

J. H. L.

August, 1913.

CONTENTS

ILLUSTRATIONS AND MAP

The author is indebted to the courtesy of His Excellency the
Japanese Ambassador for the illustrations of the Emperor Komei
and of Marquis Inouye.

INTRODUCTION

In the 7th century of the Christian era, Japan, as one incident in the general assimilation of Chinese civilisation which then took place, adopted the Chinese calendar, in which years are counted in chronological periods of irregular length, distinguished from each other by specific names—*nengo* or year names. In 1872, subsequent to the abandonment of the Chinese in favour of the European system as the foundation of the national civilisation, the old calendar was replaced by the Gregorian, though not in its entirety. A formal recognition of the Christian era would have been inconsistent with the reverence that was due to the Emperor as the acknowledged descendant of the Gods of Heaven, and to the national religion of which he was the head, and it was therefore decided that while days and months should henceforth be reckoned on the Western model, the old system of year-counting by *nengo* should be retained. Under it a name, usually one of good omen, such as "Great Honour," "Heavenly Virtue," "Tranquil Peace," "Great Prosperity," was chosen at the beginning of each period

L.   1 and the successive years were described as the first, second, etc. years of that period until the time came when it was arbitrarily terminated and a new one adopted. There was not even a remote approximation to uniformity in the length of the periods. Many only continued for one year, while three exceeded 20 and one 30 years.

In the year following the accession of the late Emperor the occurrence of his birthday was signalised by the inauguration of a new period to which the name of Meiji—Enlightened Government—was given. It was, at the same time, decreed that in future there should be only one chronological period in each reign and that it should coincide with the length of the reign, with the exception that, as a new period has, through all ages, always been reckoned from the first day of the year of its adoption, each should in future begin on the 1st of January preceding the sovereign's accession and close on the 31st of December preceding his death. The period of Meiji —the longest in history—dates from January 25th, 1868, that being New Year's Day under the old (Chinese) calendar, till December 31st, 1911, and is almost synchronous with the late Emperor's reign. In this volume we propose to tell the story of the evolution of Japan from an unknown and impotent Asiatic state into one of the acknowledged Powers of the world, which took place during the period of Meiji, in the reign of the Emperor Mutsu Hito. It is the story of one of the most eventful reigns of any period or of any nation in the world's history, a story which is full of the most pregnant lessons of what can be achieved by an intelligent and courageous people, working with whole-hearted patriotism, under the leadership of a liberal and enlightened sovereign.

CHAPTER I

HISTORICAL SKETCH

BEFORE proceeding with our main task it is necessary that a short sketch of the history and polity of Japan should be given in order that our readers may be enabled to have a clear understanding of the social and political conditions of the Empire at the beginning of Meiji. The first Emperor was Jimmu Tenno, who founded the Empire and ascended the throne in the year 660 B.C., little more than a century later than the founding of Rome. From him, all the subsequent occupants of the throne traced their descent in an unbroken line, and as Jimmu was the direct descendant, in the fifth genera-tion, of the Sun Goddess (Tenshō Daijin), who herself sprang from the creators of Heaven and Earth, all

1—2

his successors have claimed through him a divine
descent, a claim which has been accepted with unquestioning faith by their subjects in all times, which
the most extreme spirit of modern materialism has
not yet affected, and which is as devoutly acknowledged to this day by the most advanced student of
Huxley or Schopenhauer as it was by any of the
sages of old.

Jimmu's successors, throughout twelve centuries,
were all sovereigns in reality as well as in name, all
taking an active and vigorous share in their government, but from the seventh century of the Christian
era they permitted the executive power to fall into
the hands of the leading family among their courtiers,
the Fujiwara, who, like the Emperors themselves,
claimed divine origin, their remote ancestor having
descended from Heaven in the train of Jimmu's
progenitor, the Sun Goddess's grandson ; they also,
like the Emperors, survive to this day. For four
hundred years the Fujiwara conserved to themselves
all the executive authority of the realm until it was
wrested from them by the leaders of a race of soldiers,
who, while the later generations of the Fujiwara
were, in the ease and luxury of the Court at Kioto,
sinking into the condition of idle and incapable
voluptuaries, had been hardened by continuous
military service against the Ainu, the savage autoch-
thons of Japan, in those days still numerous and

powerful on the northern frontiers of the lands that had been colonised by the followers of Jimmu and their descendants. The greatest of these leaders was Yoritomo, who succeeded at the close of the twelfth century in making himself dictator of the Empire, under the title of Sei-i-tai-Shogun or "Barbarian-repressing-great-General," which was conferred on him by the Emperor. The title, abbreviated in common use into Shogun, was one which had previously been frequently conferred on generals in command of armies in the field, but it signified only military authority and it lapsed with the termination of the special command for which it was given. Yoritomo gave it a new significance. He assumed not only the military but the civil power and retained the title for life. He established his residence at Kamakura, a town about 30 miles from Tokio, which quickly grew into a large and populous city and became the real capital of the Empire while Kioto, the home of the legitimate Emperors, was only so in name. There he administered, as the *de facto* sovereign, the government of the Empire while the provinces were held and governed by his relatives and adherents, soldiers who had fought by his side and who owed all their fealty to him alone.

This was the beginning of the systems of dual government and of feudalism in Japan which lasted from the time of Yoritomo (1192—1199) until the accession of the late Emperor. At Kioto there was always the Emperor, the legitimate sovereign, the acknowledged source of all authority and the sole fountain of honour, surrounded by a small retinue of courtiers, who were known as Kuge, many of whom sprang from the Imperial family, and all of whom claimed an origin and descent that were only less illustrious than those of the Emperor. Both Emperors and court were entirely dependent on the Shoguns for their means of support, which were for many long centuries provided with such parsimony, that all were practically sunk in abject poverty. On the other side, the Shogun's courts, first at Kamakura and afterwards at Yedo, with an interval between the two at Kioto, in the very shadow of the Emperor's own palace, were maintained in the utmost Imperial splendour; the national executive was entirely in the hands of the Shoguns and their ministers, and all the land in the provinces was parcelled among feudal lords—the daimio—the majority of whom sprang from soldiers of fortune who were rewarded by successive dynasties of the Shoguns with the grants of large estates, the spoils of almost unceasing civil war.

Yoritomo's own direct descendants did not long hold the great office which their progenitor had won. It fell in turn to other military adventurers during the succeeding four centuries, the last and the greatest of whom was Tokugawa Iyeyasu who became Shogun at the beginning of the seventeenth century. The system, inaugurated by Yoritomo, was brought to its highest perfection by Iyeyasu, who, in the measures he took to secure the retention of the Shogunate in his own family and the peace of the realm, showed that he was a constructive statesman of the highest order of genius, and he was ably followed by some of his earliest successors. So successful were he and they, that throughout 260 years, during which his descendants occupied the throne of the Shoguns at Yedo, their authority was never once questioned and the country under their government, which, for five centuries prior to the accession of Iyeyasu, had been almost continuously desolated by civil war, fought with no less bitterness and savage cruelty than those which characterised the wars of Europe in the same periods, enjoyed profound and unbroken peace, and its people, according to the descriptions of European writers, who saw and studied them, should have been one of the happiest in the world.

To this picture there was another side. During the last half of the sixteenth and the first quarter of the seventeenth centuries Japan freely admitted to her harbours European ships, which found their way to the Far East, and Portuguese, Spanish, Dutch and English traders were in turn welcomed by her. Jesuit and other missionaries of the Roman Catholic

Church followed the first Portuguese and Spanish
traders and their proselytising efforts, carried on
with equal zeal and ability, met with such success
that, within one century from the landing of the first
missionary, there were said to have been over a million
native converts to Christianity of all classes of the
people. Unfortunately the zeal of the missionaries
outran their discretion and gave rise to the suspicion
that proselytism was merely an antecedent step to
territorial aggression threatening the political independence of the Empire, and as the suspicion grew
to certainty, the whole attitude of the Government
changed both to Christianity and to Europeans.
Christianity was extirpated by persecution as ruthless
as that of Nero. Missionaries were put to death or
expelled. Traders too were expelled, an exception
being made only in favour of the Dutch, a small colony
of whom were permitted to remain under the most
humiliating conditions, closely interned in the little
island of Desima in the harbour of Nagasaki, where
they carried on a trade which, though hampered by
vexatious restrictions, brought them enormous profits.
All other Europeans were forbidden to approach the
shores of Japan or to land on pain of death. And
not only were Europeans forbidden to land in Japan,
but Japanese were, under equally severe penalties,
forbidden to go abroad. None who did so was
permitted to return. Throughout the middle ages

the Japanese had shown themselves bold and adventurous seamen, making their way both as pirates and traders not only to China and Siam, but in some instances across the Pacific to Mexico. Now they were forbidden by their own authorities to build any ship larger in burthen than 500 Koku (50 tons) and from the day on which the edict which forbade them was issued their traditional maritime spirit was gone, and the national seclusion, which it was the policy of the early Tokugawas to effect, was complete.

For 220 years Japan was cut off from all the world. She had her own high degree of social and artistic civilisation, refined and picturesque in all its elements, but while Europe was advancing with giant strides in industrial, military and political science, Japan stood still and her internal state in the middle of the nineteenth century showed no material advance on what it had been in the early part of the seventeenth. She was contented in herself and with her own acquirements and neither knew nor cared for aught that was happening in the outer world.

Internally the country was crushed under one of the most iron systems of feudalism that the world has ever seen. The Shogun was the feudal superior, though nominally only as the mandatory of the Emperor. A third of the whole Empire was under his direct rule and the revenues were paid into his Treasury. The remainder was shared among 260 feudal lords, all of whom varied in strength, wealth and influence in proportion to the extent of their domains, but all alike enjoyed complete legislative and executive autonomy within their own boundaries, an autonomy which did not even exclude the right of coinage. All maintained armies of hereditary soldiers —samurai—whose allegiance was due only to their own immediate feudal lords, for whose sake every samurai was always ready to sacrifice without a murmur life, liberty, name, family or property. Each lord, in his turn, owed allegiance to the Shogun, from whom he received his investiture on succession, whose approval he had to obtain in marriage and adoption, and to whom he was obliged to render military service when called upon. All lived in regal splendour and independence in fortified castles on their own estates, and in no less splendour in great palaces in Yedo, where they were obliged to pass part of each year. The sole occupations of the samurai were those of arms, literature and the administration of their lords' estates and revenues, and both daimio and samurai combined to form the governing and aristocratic class and with their families numbered some two million souls. Beneath them, divided by an unfathomable social gulf, across which none could pass, was the subject and plebeian class, divided into three orders, farmers, artisans and traders, in number about thirty millions, whose sole lot in life was to minister to the well-being and luxury of their superiors.

The general characteristics of the Japanese people were then such that there is scarcely a word which Buckle wrote in the second chapter of his *History of Civilization* on the physical and moral conditions of the ancient peoples of India, Egypt, Mexico or Peru, which *mutatis mutandis* might not have been applied to those of the people of Japan. On the part of the upper class there was the most autocratic use of despotic power; on that of the lower the most servile subservience in every incident of life. Slavery, except perhaps in prehistoric times, never existed as a recognised institution in Japan, but practically speaking, less than sixty years ago, slavery, abject slavery, was the natural state of the great body of the people. They counted for nothing. They not only had no voice in the management of the public affairs of the state, the province, or the city, but their liberty, their property, and even their lives were held at the absolute disposal of their immediate rulers. Their occupations, their dress, their residences were all rigidly prescribed for them; on them fell the entire financial burthens of the state and their sole functions were to labour for the comfort and luxury of the upper classes and to render to them an absolute and unquestioning obedience. The "habits of tame and servile submission were generated among them" and extended through successive generations had their invariable result in that the history of the world affords no more striking instance of an abjectly spiritless race thàn that of the Japanese lower classes only sixty years ago. They spoke in subdued tones, with bent backs and eyes on the ground : they would scarcely dare to strike a blow even in the defence of their own lives and families, and all the history of Japan does not furnish one single instance of their having "turned upon their rulers, of any war of classes, of any popular insurrection, of even one great popular conspiracy."

As subjection made the lower classes abjectly servile so did despotic power and immunity from all the burthens of life render the aristocratic class tyrannical and cruel. The samurai of Japan have been quoted in England as models of everything that is most noble in man, as chivalrous, frugal, brave, courteous, loyal, patriotic, self-sacrificing. They were all that theoretically, and actually so in many individual cases, but foreigners in Japan, fifty years ago, conceived very different ideas of them as a class. Sir Rutherford Alcock, our first minister to Japan, a keen observer, a man of the world, a careful student, who knew the Japan of his day, calls them "Swash-bucklers, swaggering blustering bullies, many cowardly enough to strike an enemy in the back or cut down an unarmed and inoffensive man, but ever ready to fling their own lives away in accomplishing a revenge or carrying out the behests of their chief." Even contemporaneous writers of their own class in Japan described them as ignorant, cruel, dissolute and idle. They treated the classes below them with the utmost contempt and brutality. Their patriotism and loyalty were local not national, were given entirely to their immediate feudal chiefs and not to the sovereign, and jealousy among rival clans would always have been a serious obstacle to national union, even in defence of the country against foreign aggression.

Such were the conditions of the people of Japan in the closing years of the Tokugawa regime. They were all, daimio, samurai and plebeians, entirely segregated from their legitimate sovereign, the Emperor, who, living in the sacred seclusion of his palace at Kioto, maintained intact the divine prestige which had been transmitted to him from his ancestors but was utterly powerless to assert himself in the administration of the Empire of which he was the nominal head. The Shogun was his Mayor of the Palace, the major-domo, who carried on the Government and who alone of all his subjects enjoyed the right of access to him. So great was the power of the Shogun, so complete its outer manifestation, both at the beginning and at the close of the Tokugawa regime, that Europeans who came to Japan invariably termed him "His Majesty." The learned Jesuits of the

16th and 17th centuries, the equally learned Dutch savants of the 18th century, and the diplomatists of the 19th century all erred alike. They heard vaguely of another Emperor who was never seen either by his own subjects or by them, not even when they visited the holy city of Kioto in which he lived, of whom they were told as a sacred being of divine origin, vested with divine prerogatives and shrouded in impenetrable mystery, but powerless as a political factor in the state, so much so that neither the Jesuit missionaries nor the Dutch traders seem ever to have made the smallest effort to enlist his influence in their favour.

On the other hand, what they termed "the Emperor," but who was in reality the Shogun, the Mayor of the Palace, was very vividly present to the eyes and thoughts of both. His authority over all the realm was undisputed. All the feudal lords, both great and small, rendered homage to him, and though exercising almost unlimited autonomy in their own domains accepted his orders with unquestioning obedience. He had great wealth of his own, the yearly revenue from his family estates amounting to eight millions sterling in an age when the purchasing power of money was manifold what it now is. He had at his call an immense army of devoted samurai, he had a council of able ministers and he lived in imperial splendour, that was apparent to all, both

The Emperor Komei

natives and foreigners, in the great city of Yedo which in size, wealth and population far outshadowed the ancient and venerated capital of Kioto. To the Jesuits, fresh from the splendours of Rome, Madrid or Lisbon, his palace seemed in its grandeur, glittering with gold, "like an enchanted palace," and when attended by a great and stately escort he made royal progresses beyond its walls, the streets were all cleared of everything that could offend his sight; the upper windows of all houses closed so that none could look down on him; no fires could be lighted for two days beforehand lest the sky should be obscured, and all people humbly prostrated themselves on the ground as he passed by.

When Europeans once more made their appearance on the shores of Japan, no longer as abject suppliants like the Dutch, but demanding ingress as a right and prepared to support their demands with irresistible force, the Emperor was still a myth in their eyes. The Shogun was the *de facto* sovereign with whom they had to deal and as far as they knew, in their ignorance of the history and institutions of Japan, he was also the *de jure* sovereign. In Perry's treaty he was described as "the August Sovereign of Japan," and in the first English treaty—that of Admiral Stirling concluded in 1854—as "His Imperial Highness, the Emperor": in Lord Elgin's Treaty of 1858, as "His Majesty the Tycoon," and in the

Prussian Treaty of 1861, as "Seine Majestät der
Taikun." The title "Tycoon" or more properly
"Taikun" was a new one adopted from China. Its
literal signification is "Great Lord."

The new treaties came into force in 1858. The
ports of Yokohama, Nagasaki and Hakodate were
opened to foreign trade and residence. Diplomatic
representatives of the Treaty Powers took up their
residence in Yedo and their countrymen began to
live and trade at the opened ports. The Shogun
apparently retained all his power and influence and
the country was governed by his ministry with whom
alone the foreign diplomatists had any direct relations. But a revolution had already begun which
was destined within one decade to destroy utterly
the political fabric that had lasted for more than
seven centuries and to restore to the legitimate
Emperor all the executive functions that were his
undoubted constitutional prerogative.

CHAPTER II

RESTORATION OF THE EMPEROR

IYEYASU in his old age devoted himself to the
study and encouragement of literature. His grandson, the feudal lord of the province of Mito and the
chief of one of the Go Sankei, the three families in

which was vested the succession to the Shogunate in the event of failure of the direct line, inherited all his grandfather's literary tastes and, unlike him, was able to devote his whole life to their cultivation. Iyeyasu favoured the study of the Confucian classics and other masterpieces of the ancient literature of China. The Lord of Mito, on the other hand, was attracted by the ancient records of Japan which told the story of the creation and of the divine descent of the Emperors. Under his patronage, the great scholars whom he gathered around him in his province from all parts of the Empire compiled the *Dai-Nihon-Shi*, the *History of Great Japan* from the accession of the mythical Emperor Jimmu in 660 B.C. to the abdication in 1414 A.D. of Go Komatsu, the ninety-ninth Emperor of the line. This great work was completed in 1715, and it was followed, one hundred years later, by the *Nihon Guaishi*, the *External History of Japan*, which told the true history of the Shogunate, from its foundation by Yoritomo in the 12th century down to the accession of Iyeyasu. Both works were eagerly read by scholars throughout the Empire. Their whole spirit was that the Emperor is the true and only legitimate sovereign, the lineal descendant of the Gods of Heaven by whom Japan was created, the first and best of all the lands on earth ; that to him alone the unquestioning allegiance of every loyal Japanese is due ; and that the

Shoguns were usurpers, who, themselves of no higher degree than the other feudal lords, had vested themselves with the supreme executive authority by the power of the sword.

These doctrines were eagerly imbibed by the greatest of the feudal lords, who were traditional enemies of the House of Tokugawa but had yielded to its superior strength and to the irresistible military and political genius of Iyeyasu. Prominent among them were the chiefs of the great southern fiefs of Choshiu and Satsuma. They were themselves hereditary foes but both had been long fretting under the domination of the Shogun with all its attendant disabilities, and their impatience was intensified by the incapacity and sloth of several of Iyeyasu's later successors. Both hated each other but both hated their Tokugawa oppressor still more, and only awaited a plausible cause and a favourable opportunity for combining their arms against him and enlisting the aid of other feudal chiefs who were in the same position as themselves. Both cause and opportunity were furnished by the arrival of Europeans and their demand that the country should be opened to them.

While the great sea Powers of Europe were too fully occupied in their own international jealousies and in the acquisition and expansion of colonies comparatively near at hand to bestow even a thought on a remote and unknown island Empire of whose people and resources they were entirely ignorant, Japan had acquired interest and importance in the eyes of the United States of America. The Western States of the Union were growing in commercial value, and it was already foreseen that the Pacific might become a highway of trade between America and the rich and populous Empire of China. Japan lay in the ocean fairway between the two countries and it was of vital interest to American shipping, trading between them, that it should have the right of access to Japanese harbours. The United States Government, entirely unhampered by either domestic or foreign complications, determined therefore to establish intercourse with the Japanese, to induce them to enter into treaty relations, by persuasion if possible, if not by force, and thus secure guarantees for the future protection and assistance of United States ships when in Japanese waters. The mission was entrusted to Commodore Perry and successfully carried out by him, and on the 31st of March 1854, Japan signed her first formal treaty with a Western Power.

Along with the revival of loyalty to the Emperor another doctrine, ancillary to it, had also won many disciples. This was that Japan is the Land of the Gods, and only those who are children of the Gods are worthy to dwell in it, that the presence of outer Barbarians is sacrilege to be avoided at all cost and

2—2

at all risks. When Perry arrived, "Peace and Prosperity of long duration had," it was said, "enervated
the spirit, rusted the armour and blunted the swords
of the Samurai" and incapacitated them for military
service against the Barbarians in their heavily-armed
ships. The Shogun, only too conscious of the national
impotency to resist the demand that was made in no
uncertain language, yielded, and by doing so at once
became a traitor to the Emperor and the country.
The cry was raised "Sonno Joi," "Honour the Emperor
and expel the Barbarians," and it was eagerly taken
up by the leaders and clansmen of the Satsuma,
Choshiu and other great southern fiefs, and made by
them a pretext for initiating hostilities against the
hated Government beneath which they had so long
cowered.

The Emperors had, as already explained, been,
with a very few striking exceptions, political nullities
throughout the whole existence of the Shogunate.
It happened that the Emperor Komei, the 120th
of his line, who occupied the throne at this period,
formed one of these exceptions. He had never fallen
into the physical and mental incapacity of his fore-
runners and was now in the very prime of early
manhood. All the revived traditions of his house
and country had entered deeply into his heart, and
he hated both the Shogunate, by which he knew he
had been despoiled of his Imperial prerogatives, and

with a still more mastering passion the foreigners, who were now polluting his country with their presence. His hatred against both Shogun and foreigner was intensified by the thought that the treaties which the former had traitorously signed, under which the foreigners lived within his dominions, were a new and further outrage on his prerogatives, a violation of the constitutional principle, which had existed throughout all ages, that great national changes required the formal sanction of the Emperor, nominal though his authority was. The indignation of both Emperor and Court was strong, and all their sympathy was with the great feudal chiefs who were now in open rebellion.

We need not enter into the details of the civil war, a war which was fought with great bitterness, much bloodshed and varying fortune. In the end, the revolutionaries were completely successful, but before that climax was reached the deaths occurred within a very short interval of the two principal figures of the times. In September 1866, Iyemochi, the fourteenth Shogun of the Tokugawa line, died and was succeeded by Yoshinobu, who was destined to be the last of the dynasty. Iyemochi was little more than a boy, who was entirely in the hands of his ministers and vassals. Yoshinobu, on the other hand, had already, on his accession, arrived at manhood, and was fully capable of forming his own opinion and exercising his judgment on the changing conditions of Japanese life and politics. The death of Iyemochi was followed within six months by that of the conservative and bigoted Emperor Komei, and the reverse of what had occurred in the case of the Shogunate happened in regard to the succession to the Imperial throne.

While Perry's mission was being organised at Washington an event took place in Kioto which was destined to have even a greater influence on Japan's history than Perry's eventful mission. On the 3rd of November, 1852, a son was born to the Emperor, his mother being the Lady Nakayama, the daughter of a cadet branch of the Fujiwara family, one of the Jugo (morganatic wives) who, from time immemorial, have been united to the Emperor by ties only one degree less formal and no less binding than those which unite him to the Empress. In accordance with custom and law, the child at once became the legitimate son of the Emperor and of the Empress, but it was not till he was eight years old, and all hope had gone of the Empress bearing a son of her own, that he was proclaimed Imperial Crown Prince and heir-apparent to his father's throne. The Emperor Komei, as already indicated, was a man of strong character and will, saturated with political convictions which he was determined to enforce in so far as his circumstances permitted. His successor was the boy whose birth

The Emperor Yoshi Hito

has just been described, and who was not yet fifteen years of age. He had been brought up in the rigidly conservative atmosphere of the Court, subject to the influence of his father and of the courtiers in the closest attendance on him, but he had had the advantage of personal tutors, one at least of whom already saw that Japan's days of isolation were over and that a new era had dawned. Whatever his own boyish sentiments may have been, he was of necessity dependent on the advice of his ministers during the earlier years of his reign. They were at his accession still all outwardly devoted to the policy of his father, the expulsion at all costs of the hated foreigners from the divine land of the Gods, but two events which had occurred during the lifetime of the Emperor Komei had already convinced even the most bigoted among them that in Japan's condition at the time, ignorant as she was of all the modern science of war and divided by bitter feuds among her own people, the successful accomplishment of this policy was hopeless.

The two events were the bombardment of Kagoshima, the capital city of the great Satsuma fief, by the British fleet in 1863, and the bombardment of Shimonoseki, the stronghold of the equally great Choshiu fief, by the allied fleets of Great Britain, France, the United States and Holland in 1865. The object of the first was to exact reparation for the murder of a British subject; of the second to open to foreign shipping the Straits of Shimonoseki which the ruler of the fief had determined to keep closed. Satsuma and Choshiu were the two most powerful fiefs in the Empire. Both had warmly and enthusiastically adopted the exclusionist policy though from different motives, Choshiu being a sincere and wholehearted advocate of it, while Satsuma used it mainly as a means of embarrassing the Tokugawa Government. Both suffered severely, Satsuma in the loss of ships and men, and in the destruction of a great part of the capital—it may be mentioned that the British fleet did not come out of the action scatheless—and Choshiu in the silencing of all the forts on the narrow straits which he had fondly believed to be impregnable, and in the defeat of the flower of his army by the allied forces landed from the fleets after the silencing of the forts. The results were the same in both cases. The feudatories recognised Japan's military impotency against the great Powers of the West, and thinking men learned the great lesson that national unity was essential to national safety, and that one of the first requisites to national unity was the abolition of the dual form of government of Emperor and Shogun.

The lessons learned at such cost by Satsuma and Choshiu were soon imbibed, not only by other great feudatories, but even by some of the Imperial courtiers

at Kioto. They could not however as yet be openly
acknowledged. The civil war was still in progress.
The Emperor Komei was still obstinate in his old convictions, and the old cry of "Expel the Barbarians"
was still the most potent charm for all the enemies
of the Shogunate, few of whom were even yet enlightened enough to understand, still less to acknow-
ledge, the new position in which Japan found herself.
Two years later, the death of the Emperor removed
one great obstacle, and then a far-reaching step was
taken by a third feudatory, the lord of Tosa, a fief
that was inferior in wealth and strength only to
Satsuma and Choshiu. He addressed a memorial to
the new Shogun, pointing out Japan's helplessness
in the face of foreigners and its own internal disorganisation, urging as the only remedy the complete restoration of the executive authority to the
Imperial Government in whom alone it could be
legally vested.

The memorial expressed only what was in the
Shogun's own thoughts, and urged a course of action
which he himself had already seen to be inevitable.
On the one side were the Court and the great majority
of the feudatories plotting for his fall, many of the
latter in arms against him, and all outwardly clamor-
ing for the expulsion of the foreigners. On the other
were the diplomatic representatives of the Foreign
Powers, pressing him to fulfil the obligations he had

undertaken in the treaties, and, in their ignorance
of the political conditions of Japan, utterly unable to
appreciate or make any allowance for the domestic
difficulties which surrounded him. The lessons taught
by the bombardments of Kagoshima and Shimonoseki,
though the most bitter domestic enemies of his own
house had been the sufferers in both cases, had not
been wasted on him. He saw that a country divided
as Japan was into local principalities, no one of which
interested itself in any calamities that might befall
its neighbour, among whom there were no common
interests, where all patriotism was local and not
national, could have no hope of being able to with-
stand foreign aggression, and he knew enough of the
fate of India and of the spoliation of China to be
assured that foreign aggression was an imminent
danger so long as Japan was helpless to defend herself. No national unity could be attained while the
dual system of government continued, and yielding
to the teaching of his youth, while he was still a cadet
of the house of Mito, in which the doctrine of loyalty
to the Emperor had its birth, to the experience of his
manhood, and to the high ideal of self-sacrificing
patriotism which was the product of both, worn out
too by the helplessness of his position and all the
heart burnings and humiliations entailed by his in-
ability to coerce his domestic enemies on the one side
or to carry out the engagements his Government had

made with foreign powers on the other, he resigned his office of Shogun and restored the national executive to its proper source, the Emperor.

By doing so he not only surrendered the supreme executive authority of the Empire, which had been held by his family for 260 years, but ended the dual system of government, which had lasted from the 12th century. All this occupied little more than one year. It was on the 19th of September, 1866, that the fourteenth Shogun died, and on the 6th of January, 1867, Yoshinobu was nominated his successor. The Emperor Komei died and was succeeded by his only son, Mutsu Hito, on the 3rd of February, 1867, and it was on the 9th of November in the same year that the new Emperor received the Shogun's resignation and assumed in its complete reality the authority which had belonged to his remote ancestors. It was on the day he did so that the foundation stone of modern Japan was laid. Much was yet to be accomplished, more blood was to be shed before Japan entered on the paths of social, political and industrial reform on which she was destined to make such great advances, but the first step had been accomplished and the promoters of the revolution were free to take in the name of the boy Emperor, who had just ascended the throne, such measures as were incumbent to ensure the consolidation and permanency of the new Government.

CHAPTER III

REFORMS IN FOREIGN AND DOMESTIC POLICY

THE reader will have gathered from the preceding chapters that while the main object of the promoters of the Restoration was the destruction of the Shogunate and the revival of the Imperial regime, they had utilised the cry of "expel the barbarian," in order to cement in one common bond of union all the fighting forces of the Empire not bound to the Tokugawa cause by ties of consanguinity or material interest. They had encouraged the fanatics who abounded everywhere in the exercise of their hatred to the foreigner, seeing how much it contributed to the complications of the sorely-harassed Shogunate in its last years. The late Emperor had, in formal rescripts, conveyed his unqualified approval to the Satsuma and Choshiu fiefs, when they fought against the fleets of Great Britain and the allied Powers, and public sentiment had no less approved of the deeds of the many assassins by whom unoffending Europeans were over and over again cruelly and savagely murdered. Twice, almost in the very heart of the Shogun's capital, the British Legation was attacked at night by large bands of armed samurai, with the avowed object of murdering all its inmates, and the

assailants were regarded as devoted patriots by all
their compeers. The officials of the Foreign Legations,
the only foreigners who resided in Yedo, had all to
be closely guarded both when within their Legations
and when they ventured outside the walls, and so
insecure was the position of all Europeans in Japan,
that large garrisons of English and French troops
were quartered by their governments in Yokohama
to afford to the traders resident there the protection
which it was believed the Shogunate had not the
power to secure.

All who had shared the anti-foreign sentiment and
had fought for their beliefs, fondly believed that the
moment the Emperor regained his own an anti-foreign
campaign would be at once instituted under the
Emperor's banner, and they were as ready to give
their swords to it as they had been to the overthrow of the Shogun. But while the cry of "expel
the foreigner" had been openly used to the very last,
so long as the Shogun was a power to be feared, a
change had during the last years of the struggle taken
place in the minds of the leaders of the movement.
The two most powerful fiefs who took an active part
in it had received severe lessons of the consequences
of indulging in armed resistance to European powers.
Some of the courtiers had also imbibed more liberal
sentiments, under the influence of the leaders of the
fiefs, and there was a sufficiently influential body of

capable men around the young Emperor to mould his opinions and to develop in his name, while he was still too young to take the direct personal control of state affairs which was his right, the policy that they now believed was essential to the future integrity and progress of Japan. This policy meant a complete subversal of all that they had hitherto openly advocated, but it was at once boldly and publicly adopted.

On the 8th of February, 1868, a nobleman of high rank in the Court delivered to the Diplomatic Representatives of the foreign powers a formal document bearing the sign manual of the Emperor and sealed with "The Seal of Great Japan" for transmission to their Governments, in which the Emperor announced his intention of thenceforward exercising supreme authority both in the internal and external affairs of the country and of substituting in the treaties his own title for that of the Tycoon. This was followed a week later by a public rescript in which it was proclaimed that "intercourse with foreign countries shall in future be carried on in accordance with the public law of the whole world," and, as a first onward step on this path, an invitation soon followed to the Representatives to visit Kioto and be received in audience by His Majesty.

Kioto had been for more than a thousand years the sacred city of the Empire. It had been visited in the sixteenth and seventeenth centuries by the

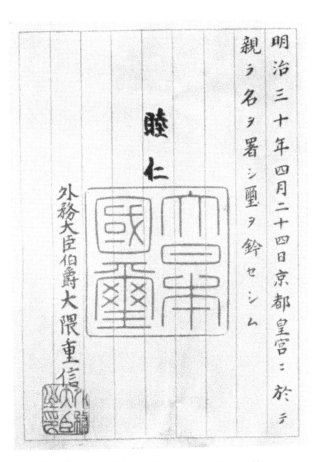

明治三十年四月二十四日京都皇宮ニ於テ

親ラ名ヲ署シ璽ヲ鈐セシム

睦仁

外務大臣伯爵大隈重信

Sign Manual and Seal of the Emperor Mutsu Hito

Jesuit missionaries, and Xavier and many of his disciples had openly preached the Christian doctrine in its streets. The Dutch traders had passed through it when on their way from Desima on their compulsory annual missions to the Shogun's court at Yedo. But neither had ever approached the palace or dreamt of audience with its holy occupant, and the Dutch always passed through the city closely guarded as though they were prisoners. Now the foreigners, who a very few years before had been publicly designated by the late Emperor as "Sea pirates," "Ugly Barbarians," and "Foul beasts," were not only to be admitted to the holy city but were to be received in person by the direct descendant of the Gods of Heaven; they were to approach him erect and not humbly on their knees with foreheads touching the ground, and to gaze upon him with no intervening screen between him and them, such as had hitherto veiled his sacred person from the eyes even of the highest and noblest of his own people, even of the Great Lord, the Shogun, when at the very summit of his might and grandeur.

It is difficult even for a thinking Japanese of modern days to appreciate the significance of this event or to realise the profound impression which it created on those who had fought and schemed for the renewal of Japan's time-honoured seclusion. The ceremony was destined not to pass without its tragedy, one of the many which darkened those days of our intercourse with Japan. When Sir Harry Parkes, the British representative, who had been the first among his colleagues to recognise the new Government and to give it his strong moral support, was on his way to the palace, two fanatics, maddened at the desecration of the Emperor and of the city, suddenly attacked his English escort and inflicted severe wounds on ten of the men composing it, before they were themselves killed or disabled.

The audience had to be postponed till the following day, but the incident, unhappy and tragic as it was, was not without its good results. It gave the young Emperor, who was receiving Europeans for the first time, not only in his own life but in all the long history of his dynasty, and whose mind was no doubt full of curiosity, an opportunity for expressing, with the sympathetic tact and dignity which characterized him in after life, his regret at what had happened and of manifesting his desire to prevent its recurrence. Hitherto every samurai who murdered a European thought that he was putting his sword, his most treasured possession, to the noblest use he could make of it and that he was performing a service to his gods, his Emperor and his country. If he was brought to justice and had to pay the penalty of his act, both law and custom permitted him to be his own executioner and to find death in a way that brought no dishonour on either him or his relatives, which was in fact the consummation of martyrdom. An Imperial rescript was issued within a few days ordering the nation :—

to obey His Majesty's will in the fulfilment of the Treaties with Foreign Countries in accordance with the rules of International Law,

and declaring that :—

all persons in future guilty of murdering foreigners or of committing acts of violence towards them will be acting in opposition to His Majesty's express orders and be the cause of national misfortune. They will therefore be punished in proportion to the gravity of their offence, and their names, if samurai, will be erased from the roll.

The last clause involved not only social degradation to the offender and his family, but a humiliating death to the former at the hands of the public executioner. Thenceforward the murderer of a foreigner lost the character of a martyr and became a common criminal like any robber or thief. From that day outrages of this nature entirely ceased. Europeans have, it is true, since been murdered by natives in Japan, but these have been cases of sordid crime such as occur in any country, and in none were the murderers actuated solely by political or religious motives.

Amidst all these indications of the new policy of peace within and of good will to all men without the Empire, one dark spot was allowed to continue. It

was an element of the domestic policy of the Tokugawas to conceal the provisions of the criminal laws
from the nation. They believed that people were
more likely to abstain from crime when they were
ignorant of, than they would be if they knew, the
utmost penalty by which their crime was punishable.
One exception was made in the observance of this
policy. In all the principal streets of every great
city, in every village and at intervals along every
high road, public notice-boards were erected in conspicuous form and places on which the great standing
laws of the Empire, the laws which are the foundation
of society and government, were proclaimed to all
who passed. They were very few in number. They
prohibited insurrection, conspiracy, murder, arson
and robbery, and enjoined the observance of the five
social relations which are the basis of all morality
according to the Confucian code. But the most
prominent prohibition, which stood at the very front
of the notice boards, was :—

The evil sect called Christian is strictly prohibited. Suspicious
persons should be reported to the proper officers and rewards will be
given.

These notices, including the prohibition of Christianity, were retained. The memories of the terrible
persecution at the beginning of the seventeenth
century and of the awful sufferings which it entailed
on tens of thousands of native converts had been

handed down from father to son through all the intervening years and made the very name of Christianity a subject of loathing and terror to Japanese of all classes. No anxiety to cultivate European good will or to fulfil the professions of friendship which were constantly in the mouths of the members of the new government could induce them to abolish or modify the old practice.

The foreign policy of the Emperor having been fully manifested to his people, the domestic policy remained to be declared, and it was soon seen that it was to be no less revolutionised than the foreign. As a first step the Emperor was to see and be seen by his people. He was no longer to be an Imperial Hermit, surrounded with mystic sanctity in a palace, "where he lived behind a screen, far from the outward world, from which nothing could penetrate his sacred ear." He was to learn the condition of his people by his own direct observation and as an absolute monarch to take an active share in all measures for their government and education. His first public appearance was made in a visit to Osaka, the great commercial city of Japan, twenty miles from the capital. Even then his presence among the people was more fictitious than real. Attended by an escort of over 10,000 men, he was carried in a palanquin, the bamboo blinds of which enabled him to see without himself being seen. From the shore he reviewed the beginning of the Japanese fleet. It consisted of but six ships, all converted merchant steamers, not one of which exceeded 1000 tons or 300 horse power, and not one of them could yet be called his, all being owned by one or other of the great fiefs. The Tokugawas possessed other and more formidable ships, manned by officers and men who had already had some professional training from British officers, but these still lay at Yedo and they never became Imperial property. They were destined to perish at Hakodate in the last fight that was made by the Tokugawa partisans.

The task of forming the new system of administration was vigorously pursued. A council of state was formed, seven departments were founded for the administration of the various branches of the Government, and all the feudal lords (daimio) having been summoned to Kioto, the Emperor in their presence and in that of all the Court nobles, assembled in solemn conclave, took what is known as the "Charter Oath," which as the foundation of modern constitutional liberty holds the same position in the history of Japan that the Magna Charta does in that of England. He promised, in the Oath, which consisted of five articles, that :—

a deliberative assembly should be formed and all measures decided by public opinion ; that civil and military government should no longer be separated and that all classes of the people should with one mind devote themselves to the national welfare; that the rights of all classes should be assured; that the uncivilized customs of antiquity should be abolished and impartiality and justice administered according to universally recognised principles; and that intellect and learning should be sought for throughout the world, so that the foundations of the Empire might be firmly established.

The programme thus outlined was both extensive and ambitious and formulated a task which could only be carried to a successful accomplishment by earnest, courageous and able statesmen. Fortunately such were not wanting. At their head were some of the Court and feudal nobles, but their aggregate did not exceed half a dozen. The rest, about fifty in all, were samurai of the four great fiefs, Satsuma, Choshiu, Tosa and Hizen, men whose ability and courage had brought them to the front ; who, though of gentle birth, were low in rank, with no advantages of birth, means or education to differentiate them from tens of thousands of their fellows. Associated with them as their guides in foreign affairs were a few young students of their own class who had the advantage of a short education in Europe. Of the first class the most prominent were Sanjo, a scion of a cadet branch of the illustrious Fujiwara family, and Iwakura of the Minamoto family, both nobles of the court, and Shimadzu Saburo, father of the Lord of Satsuma, and Yodo, Lord of Tosa, great feudal nobles. Among the samurai, the most distinguished in after life were Okubo and Saigo, samurai of Satsuma ;

Kido, a samurai of Choshiu, Okuma of Hizen and Itagaki of Tosa : while the students included Ito and Inouye of Choshiu, the first of whom may be called the constructor of Modern Japan, and the second has been one of its most distinguished statesmen and administrators. Both were mere youths in subordinate positions at the Restoration. The buttress on which all leant was the Emperor, and the new decrees, all of which were issued in his name, received from the nation the unquestioning obedience that was due to his divine prerogative.

Further reforms were soon made. A new classification of the people was adopted. The old distinction between the court and feudal nobility was abolished and both were merged in one class under the title of Kwazoku or nobles, literally Flower Families. The remainder of the samurai, irrespective of the many gradations of rank in their own fiefs, were grouped under the title of Shizoku or gentry, and the rest of the people under that of Heimin or commoners. Kioto was the acknowledged capital of the Empire, but in the last three centuries Yedo had been the seat of the executive government, and the nation had grown accustomed to regard it as the source of all active authority. It was thought that the new Imperial executive would be more readily recognised if it were administered from the same seat as had been the old, and it was therefore decided that Yedo ·

should in future be the Imperial capital, its name being changed to Tokio or Eastern capital, by which it has since been known.

This change was great and impressive, but it was thrown completely into the shade by one more profound and far-reaching which soon followed it. The Restoration had not yet entailed the abolition of feudalism. The feudal lords still continued to administer their fiefs, to exercise the same *imperium in imperio* as they had done under the Tokugawas for many preceding centuries and to retain their local autocracy unimpaired. No complete unification of the Empire under one supreme ruler could be hoped for while they did so. The lords of the four great fiefs that had been foremost in the Restoration again took the lead, and in a memorial signed by all four they voluntarily surrendered their fiefs to the Emperor and where they led all others had perforce to follow.

The memorial appeared in the Official Gazette on the 5th of March, 1869. It was at once accepted, but the mediatisation of the fiefs was not yet complete. At first their former lords were appointed Governors of what they had hitherto owned, and while they acted in the name of the Emperor they continued to collect and administer their own revenues, paying, however, a contribution to the Imperial treasury, and to retain many of their old privileges. To deprive

them of all at one stroke would have been too drastic
a step for a Government which at the time had
neither army nor money and had to rely entirely on
the goodwill of these feudatories for the enforcement
of its decrees on any among them who might prove
recalcitrant, and it was not till two years later that
the step was finally completed in its fullest measure.
Then the last blow was given to the system of
feudalism.   On the 29th of August, 1871, all the
daimio were ordered to quit their fiefs and take up
their residences for the future as private gentlemen
in Tokio, without either administrative or executive
authority, without even titles to distinguish them
from the common herd. Ten per cent. of their former
revenues were assigned to them for their support,
but they were at the same time relieved from the
maintenance of the armies of samurai who had
hitherto depended on them.   Their castles, muni-
tions and ships were handed over to the Government.
Their fiefs were converted into prefectures administered by officials, with no local prejudices, appointed
by the central Government ; all their revenues were
paid into the Imperial Treasury, from which in turn
all expenses both for their own and their samurai's
pensions and for administration were defrayed.
Uniform systems of law and currency were established, and at last a national Government, both in
name and fact, was firmly consolidated in the hands

of the Emperor and the ministers who acted for him. Then in reality began the modern Empire of Japan.

CHAPTER IV

SOCIAL REFORMS

THE civil war was terminated and peace established throughout the Empire by the subjugation of the last adherents of the Tokugawas at Hakodate in July 1869. The Emperor was firmly seated on his throne at Tokio and the acknowledged executive head of the nation, whose will none would dare to dispute. The statesmen who, supported by his divine authority, acted in his name had, throughout the long civil and military struggles which preceded his Restoration, already shown that they possessed not only determined courage but considerable political judgment. They had the sympathy, so far as it could be given without detriment to the interests of their own countries, of the foreign diplomatic representatives and therefore of the great powers of the West. But the task before them was enough to daunt the boldest courage. It was one that could only be carried to success by iron will, unflagging industry and unruffled patience. None more difficult has ever faced the statesmen of any country in the world's history. None has ever in its triumphant issue more completely realised the greatest ambitions of those who initiated it.

The social condition of the people until the abolition of feudalism has been already described. The masses, sunk in ignorance and political degradation, had to be educated and raised to the status of self-respecting citizens, equitably sharing both the obligations and privileges of their superiors. Many of the samurai still cherished their old ideas as to the expulsion of foreigners, still more the retention of their caste privileges, and they had to be taught that they must in future assume a share in the burthens of life, and become producers as well as consumers. The Government had neither army nor navy. Its treasury was empty and it had no settled revenue. The national industry was capable of little more than supplying domestic necessaries. Internal communications were destitute of all but the most primitive facilities. Neither railways, telegraphs, posts nor mercantile marine existed. Foreign trade already annually amounted in value to some millions sterling, but it was entirely in the hands of foreign middlemen, and carried on under such disabilities that the cost of conveying a bale of goods fifty miles between the seaport at which it was landed and the interior where it was consumed exceeded that of its freight between Europe and Japan, though ocean freights were then on a far higher scale than they are at the present day. Of all modern sciences, the people were almost entirely ignorant. The only exceptions were surgery and medicine, of which some knowledge had been acquired through the physicians of the Dutch factory at Nagasaki. One at least of the Western Powers pressed or threatened claims which, if yielded, would impair the territorial integrity of the Empire, and one and all insisted on the retention of the extra-territorial clauses in the treaties, which, it was now known, were a slur on Japan's prestige as a civilised and independent Power. The solution of all these problems had to be undertaken simultaneously by a ministry whose members, notwithstanding their courage and judgment, were as yet only students in domestic or international statescraft, who, in carrying out reform, had to overcome the most bigoted conservative prejudice and to face constantly the risk of assassination, a risk which, in many instances, culminated in realisation.

Fortunately for themselves and for their country, the ministers had, at this period, the aid and council of one of the ablest representatives that have served Great Britain in the Far East. Sir Harry Parkes, after a long career in China, was appointed H. M. Minister in Japan in 1865. Throughout all the political crises antecedent to the Restoration he had given his sympathy to the Imperialists and was

therefore entitled to their confidence and gratitude
when they came into power. Great Britain was then,
both as a political and economic factor, predominant
over all other Western Powers in the Far East. Her
military and naval prestige had been amply vindicated both in China and in Japan. British troops
guarded Yokohama, and both her naval and mercantile flags were seen in every port. Her consular
service was specially organised for service in Japan.
All its members were specially trained from youth
and it is to many among them that we owe the
knowledge we now possess of the language, literature,
history and economics of Japan. Her merchants were
far above those of other countries in number, wealth,
enterprise and honesty. The minister was in every
way worthy of the status of his country. He was
a man of untiring and unflagging industry, of irresistible strength of will and character, of indomitable
moral and physical courage, and of far-seeing political intelligence. His methods were often hard and
apparently tyrannical and enforced by the mailed fist
rather than gently carried through with velvet gloves,
and his object in promoting Japan's progress was
frankly avowed to be the interests of his own countrymen rather than the welfare of Japan. Great Britain
had no territorial aims. Her sole object in cultivating
intercourse with Japan was trade. The conception
of Japan as a valuable political and military ally of

Great Britain had not then even entered into the
thoughts of either Japanese or British statesmen,
but the more Japan advanced in her own material
welfare, the more was she likely to require and buy
from Great Britain, then the workshop of the world,
and that consideration was in itself sufficient to
induce the British Minister to use his best efforts
in starting and urging Japan on her career of progress according to the standards of modern European
civilisation.   In every reform that she undertook,
the British Minister was consulted.   His advice was
freely and honestly given, and throughout the first
decade of the Imperial Government's existence there
was scarcely one detail in all the great reforms that
were undertaken in which he had not a share, very
often in its initiation, always in its progress.

In another respect, the Government were equally
fortunate, though that they were so was largely
owing to the first.   It is a common text with super-
ficial English writers on Japan, that Japan reformed
herself: that her own statesmen saw of themselves the
immense material superiority of Western civilisation
to that which she owed to China and converted their
people to the same view: that all she has since
achieved in material progress is due not only to the
initiation but to the industry and perseverance of
her own sons.   Nothing could be further from the
truth.   Her entry into the paths of Western civilisation

was largely owing to the persistent goading of Sir
Harry Parkes : her subsequent achievements to the
tuition of the large band of foreign experts whom
she had the good fortune to enlist in her service,
and who served her as loyally and whole-heartedly
as they did efficiently. Most of them were still
young men when they entered her service but they
were the best products of their own countries, in
which many of them subsequently rose to high
eminence in their respective professional spheres.
Great Britain gave her the naval officers who
founded her navy and first trained its personnel.
It also gave her the engineers who constructed her
first railways, lighthouses, waterworks, mines and
telegraphs, and the founders of her mint, her bank-
ing system and her press. The United States contributed in like way to her postal and educational
systems : France to her army and dockyards and
to legal reform : Germany to her medical science
and to the creation of her constitution : and Italy
to her military arsenals. All these nations contributed their quotas to the modern development of
Japan, and to their sons is due, in no small degree,
the eminence which she has since attained in all
spheres of human life and civilisation. The teachers
had apt and industrious students, not only keen
for their own personal advancement but inflamed with
patriotic enthusiasm to serve their country and to

contribute all their best abilities in realising their Emperor's oath "to establish firmly the foundations of the Empire," but their ability, industry and enthusiasm would have had little result had they not been fortunate in their teachers.

Another class must not be overlooked if due credit is given to all who have contributed to the creation of modern Japan. From the first there was a large body of European and American missionaries in Japan, and in recent years they have increased to what may be called a small army. They include members of the Roman Catholic and Greek churches and of several scores of sects of the Protestant church, and are of all nationalities. Their success as religious propagandists has not been very great, as might naturally be expected from the obstacles they have to overcome, both of tradition and present discouragement. The statistics of the several missionary societies show numbers of converts that appear large on paper, but taken at their most favourable estimate they constitute but a drop in the great ocean of the people. But on the other hand missionaries have rendered great educational services in their schools and by the example of their lives, faithful and self-denying, have exercised no inappreciable influence on the moral regeneration of the people among whom they live.

The first step that was taken in social reform was

one that augured a new spirit of humanity in the government. It dealt with criminal law and prison administration. The criminal law of the Empire was codified and published and though it still continued to be based on its original Chinese models and torture was still retained as an incident in trials, great mitigations were made in the cruel and vindictive punishments which had hitherto characterised it. Prisons had hitherto been infernos of medieval horror. A commission was sent to visit and report on the prisons in the English colonies of Hong Kong and Singapore, and on its return, new prisons were at once constructed in which all that the commission had learnt from the English system as regards food, clothing, sanitation, cleanliness, and segregation of accused and convicted, was put in practice. In both cases these steps were only the beginning of greater and far more vital changes. The prison system was gradually improved until it reached a standard of efficiency that places it at the present day on a far higher plane of social civilisation than that of Great Britain. The duty of punishing the criminal is not lost sight of, but punishment is made subordinate to reformation. The first criminal code was only retained until a new one, compiled by a distinguished French jurist, with the assistance of Japanese experts in their own laws, could be completed. Civil codes of law were in the same way compiled by German

jurists.   In both, Western principles were adapted
to the social conditions of Japan.   Executive and
judicial functions ceased to be vested in the same
officials.   Courts of Law were established, presided
over by independent judges.   A legal profession,
manned by highly-educated practitioners, came into
being and the change that was accomplished in little
more than a quarter of a century was as great as
that of England from the 16th century to the present
day.

Other great reforms came, as did those from
China in the 6th century, "with a rush." A beginning was made in railway construction and the first
railway between Yokohama and Tokio was opened
in 1873.   The dangerous and stormy coasts were
lighted with the best modern appliances, postal
and telegraphic services introduced, medical and
engineering colleges founded, the first newspapers
made their appearance, joint stock banks began to
be a feature in commercial life, and a national mint
was established, which provided an honest uniform
coinage to replace the debased tokens previously in
circulation.   All had their beginning either in or
about the year 1871, and though their progress
towards the completeness and efficiency that now
characterize them was spread over many years and
only accomplished in the face of many disheartening
difficulties and obstacles, their way has ever been

onwards, unmarked by as much as one retrograde step. The members of the Government showed themselves to be capable and far-seeing leaders. They were willingly followed by a people who were of quick intelligence, accustomed to obey and willing to be taught. Here and there, throughout the country, spasmodic insurrections from time to time occurred, instigated by a few surviving fanatics of the old school of seclusion and Chinese bigotry, but with one exception they were insignificant and easily quelled, with little loss of life on either side, and all changes were brought about in national peace, with the hearty co-operation of the people.

Very early in her modern history it became Japan's avowed ambition to be in the Far East what England is in the West as a naval and commercial power, and English example encouraged her to create her present fine commercial marine and to start on the career of industrial and commercial progress which she now hopes, not without reason, will ere another generation has passed give her the commercial hegemony of the East. The efficiency and strength of the Japanese navy at the present day are known to all, and her mercantile flag is now seen in all the great harbours of the world. The Emperor had at first no army. His restoration to the throne and his security on it during the first years of his reign were due to the samurai of the feudatories who supported him. A national army, maintained by and owing obedience to the central Government alone, had to be created, and the duty imposed on the entire population of sharing in the military service hitherto monopolised by the samurai. In 1872, the introduction of a system of universal conscription was announced in an Imperial rescript. Under it, every male, without distinction of rank or class, was called on attaining the age of 20 years to serve with the colours for three years, followed by two periods, each of two years, in the first and second reserves, and then to continue enrolled in the territorial reserve until his fortieth year. The military machine which was thus instituted has since had four great tests. The first was in civil war, in the suppression of the Satsuma rebellion in 1877, when a well-equipped and well-trained force of 46,000 men of all arms was placed in the field. The second was in the war with China in 1894, when the full strength of the mobilised forces of 220,000 men was engaged. The third was in the Boxer campaign of 1900, when the Japanese had their first opportunity of comparing themselves with European soldiers, and the last and greatest in the war with Russia, when fully one million men were mobilised for active service. The army emerged from all these tests with triumphant success.

In Japan popular education has always been general, and though the use of the heart-breakingly

difficult Chinese script rendered the acquisition of
the arts of reading and writing infinitely more difficult, the proportion of illiterate Japanese was smaller
than in any European country. Education was, however, notwithstanding the high value placed on it,
carried on without state aid or supervision, almost
entirely in private or temple schools, and its extent
depended entirely on the means or will of the parents
of the children. After the Restoration an entirely
new departure was made. A Ministry of Public
Education was one of the departments in the newly
organised Government and with the aid of American
experts a national and compulsory system of general
education was initiated in the year 1871, under which
every form of instruction was gradually provided,
from that of the elementary schools where children
are taught the principles of morality, foremost among
them being loyalty and patriotism, and to read, write
and cypher, up to that of the universities with faculties
for the teaching of literature, philosophy and every
branch of advanced science. It was the aim of the first
reformers "that there should not be a village with
an ignorant family nor a family with an ignorant
member," and that aim has been nobly carried out,
so much so that, just as Japan's naval and military
efficiency falls behind that of no great power in the
world, the educational facilities which she provides
for her people are on a level with and in many of

their incidents above those of the most enlightened nations, and the people are worthy of what the Government has done for them. Educational authorities and teachers are alike entirely immune from one of the obstacles that has to be overcome by their colleagues in the West. Thirst for knowledge of every kind is a national characteristic, manifested even in young children, and no compulsion is required to ensure the most intense application on their part or the sacrifice to unremitting industry of the pleasures that are natural to children, youths and girls. The idler is unknown in Japanese schools and colleges, and as industry is a remedy for deficiency in aptitude, the dunce is rare.

Other reforms that can only be mentioned here, made either in 1871 or very shortly afterwards, were the adoption of the Gregorian in place of the Chinese calendar ; the abolition of all sumptuary laws, and of all the old restrictions that limited men to the occupations of their fathers and their residence to the districts in which they were born ; the emancipation of the peasants ; their release from forced labour, and their conversion from hereditary life-tenants into owners of the soil they tilled, paying to the Government an annual tax based on the value of their land, a tax which fell far below the heavy burthens they had borne under their old feudal lords but which formed the main source of the Imperial revenue till

after the China war ; and the withdrawal of all pro-
hibitions to go abroad for purposes of study, business
or pleasure.

The Emperor was still little more than a boy, but
not only was his name used in every reform that was
made, but each at its initiation and throughout the
succeeding stages of its progress was countenanced
by his presence in public.   Reforms were devised and
put into operation by his ministers, but that they
were able to convince their countrymen of their
wisdom and to carry them through all their early
stages to ultimate success was mainly due to the
public approval that was given to them by their
Emperor and to the personal interest which he invariably manifested in them.

CHAPTER V

DEVELOPMENT OF CONSTITUTIONAL GOVERNMENT

THE first clause of the Emperor's Charter Oath
declared that :—

The practice of discussion and debate shall be universally adopted
and all measures shall be decided by public opinion.

This clause is the foundation stone of the edifice
of constitutional Government in Japan.   The full
extent of the Emperor's promise was at the time far

from being realised by its framers. All the leaders of
the Restoration were still imbued with the principles
of feudalism and its class distinctions when the oath
was taken, and there was no idea of extending the
privileges which it foreshadowed beyond the class of
samurai, the only class in the nation who had then
any consciousness of political rights, or who were by
their circumstances and education capable of exercising them. This was clearly evidenced in the first
attempt that was made to carry out the promise. A
national council, to which the title of "Shugiin" or
"Assembly of Legislative Discussion" was given, was
convened at Tokio in 1869, almost exactly a year
subsequent to the date of the oath. It consisted of
276 representatives of the feudal clans, which had not
yet been mediatised, all samurai nominated by their
compeers in each clan. It was vested with no legislative authority and was in fact nothing more than a
debating club, whose discussions might take the form
of advice, but had no likelihood of influencing legislation, and its whole spirit testified the strong conservatism which was natural in its members. The assembly
met both in 1869 and in 1870, and then died a natural
death.

The Government was during the two ensuing
decades an arbitrary bureaucracy, the most prominent
factors of which were members of the Satsuma and
Choshiu fiefs, whose services at the Restoration

entitled them to claim the majority of the most important executive and legislative offices. Umbrage was naturally taken at their favoured position by the clansmen of Tosa and Hizen, who considered their own services no less deserving of recognition than those of their Satsuma and Choshiu compeers, and who felt that that recognition would have been given to them if the nation had been enabled to make its voice heard. Their discontent found a mouthpiece in Itagaki, a Tosa samurai who had been prominent throughout all the incidents of the Restoration and had filled one of the cabinet offices in the new Government. Along with other members he resigned his office in 1873, on the question of declaring war against Korea, which is described in a subsequent chapter, and thenceforward he used his freedom from all official trammels to foment an agitation, which was especially vigorous in his own province of Tosa, in favour of a parliamentary system, and was recognised as the leader of national radicalism.

In 1873 the spirit of the people was already greatly changed from what it had been in 1869 and political knowledge had begun to make its appearance among certain sections of the commoners. The press had grown in ability and influence, and, as yet unfettered by any legal restrictions on its utterances, was outspoken in favour of constitutional monarchical government and in condemnation of a tyrannical oligarchy such, as it was alleged, the Government of the Satsuma and Choshiu combination had become. Many students, who had been sent to England and the United States, were at this time returning to Japan on the completion of their studies. While abroad they had seen the prosperity and strength of the great countries of the West, and they ascribed both to the constitutional forms of government enjoyed in those countries, entirely failing to see that constitutional Government was the consequence and not the cause of what had aroused their admiration and wonder. Both in press and on platform they assailed the Government in writings and speeches of incendiary violence for its failure to carry out the pledge given by the Emperor, which they construed to mean a deliberative assembly, vested with full legislative powers, freely elected by and from the people. A situation was created which, in more recent times, has found its parallel in India and in Egypt. On the one side was a large and numerous party, principally composed of hot-headed and un-disciplined young men, with exaggerated ideas of their own knowledge and experience but strong in the leadership of a respected statesman, clamouring for a great political reform—on the other, the established Government, which, if autocratic in its methods, had earned the gratitude of the nation for steering it safely through the stress of revolution and for successfully initiating a new era of progress and improvement, one of whose most marked features was the extension of individual liberty without which the agitator's methods would have been impossible.

The Government, conscious of the utter unfitness of the people, only recently emancipated from the fetters of feudalism, for the intelligent exercise of the rights that were claimed for them, endeavoured to stem the agitation by issuing drastic laws for the control of the press and public meetings, but the laws were openly defied. The agitators, cheerfully and proudly, went to prison for long terms in scores, and their places were immediately filled by new men who continued their methods. Assassination was not only advocated but practised, and several distinguished members of the Government became its victims, while their surviving colleagues, guarded by fully-armed policemen both night and day, in the council chamber as well as in the public streets and in their own homes, led lives that were sufficient to shatter the most iron nerves. This condition of affairs continued until a temporary lull was occasioned by the great domestic crisis of the Satsuma rebellion in 1877, the last effort made by the champions of aristocratic conservatism to stem by force of arms the tide of democratic progress on which the Government was fully launched, notwithstanding its uncompromising opposition to the national agitation for a parliamentary

system. The rebellion tested the strength of the
Government to the utmost, but, while it lasted, political
agitation ceased in face of the danger which threatened
both to overthrow the Government and to restore
some of the worst features of feudalism and of the
dual executive of the Shogunate.

When the rebellion was quelled, after a campaign
that was costly both in life and treasure, the agitation
that had been temporarily stilled broke out afresh
and with intensified defiance of law and contempt of
both life and liberty. Okubo, the ablest and most
influential minister in the Government, fell by
assassins' hands in 1878. Then a sop was given by
the creation of elective local assemblies vested with
some powers of administrative finance, but, welcomed
though it was as the first step towards popular
enfranchisement, it was far from satisfying the agitators. They not only continued to increase in numbers
and in the violence of their methods, but received
a new leader, equal in ability, in the distinguished
service he had rendered at the Restoration, in the
respect in which he was held by his countrymen, and
far superior in his experience as a statesman and in
administrative ability to Itagaki, in the person of
Okuma, a samurai of Hizen, who seceded from the
Government in 1881 and enrolled himself and his
personal followers among the advocates of " Constitutional Government " in the widest sense of the term.

The Government at last yielded and shortly after Okuma's secession an Imperial rescript appeared, in which the promise was given in the Emperor's name and under his sign manual that a national parliament should be convened in 1890 "in order that the Imperial purpose of gradually establishing a constitutional form of Government might be carried out." All reason for further agitation was now gone. No one dared doubt the fulfilment of the Emperor's promise, but the hatred of the bureaucratic oligarchy whose power was still unlimited was not appeased. Outcries against it continued and had to be stifled with the same means of imprisonment, police suppression of public meetings, arbitrary suspension of newspapers, and expulsion of dangerous characters from the capital under drastic Peace Preservation Acts. A large number of the most prominent agitators suffered imprisonment or expulsion, but the Government, undisturbed by all the uproar around it, calmly continued on its way. The reforms, initiated in 1871, for the material and social improvement of the nation were steadily advanced and the national finances, which seemed at one time to presage inevitable bankruptcy, were rehabilitated and placed on a sound basis. Ito, who, after Okubo's death and Okuma's secession, was by far the ablest member of the Government, was sent to Europe to investigate the constitutional models which it afforded,

Prince Ito

and soon after his return the whole administrative system of the Government was changed and recast so as to resemble in some degree that of Great Britain. A cabinet was created consisting of ten ministers of state, nine of whom were chiefs of the principal executive departments with a Minister President or Prime Minister, who held no portfolio, at their head. All held their appointments solely at the will of the Emperor, were nominated by and directly responsible to him. The change was made so as to render the form of government more suitable to a country which was shortly to have parliamentary institutions, and, to prepare still further for these institutions, another step was taken which made a great change in social life. Ito had learned in Europe that a House of Peers was a necessary part of any parliamentary system and a peerage was created from which the House could be formed.

The old nobility of Japan has been described in a previous chapter. None in any country in the world exceeds it either in the long, unbroken genealogy of its members or in the distinguished position they occupied in their country, whether as the retinue of the Imperial court or as great feudal lords who were quasi-sovereigns in their own domains. When the mediatisation of the fiefs was completed in 1871, the old individual titles of both court and feudal nobles were taken away and, as no new ones were given, they had no longer names or titles to distinguish them from their fellow subjects. This continued until the year 1884, when the Emperor established the "Five orders of Nobility," the titles of which were taken from China, and are translated as Prince, Marquis, Count, Viscount and Baron. All the heads of the old noble houses were included in one or other of these ranks according to their former degrees, but with them were associated many who, born simple samurai, merited the Emperor's recognition by their services to the state at or since the Restoration. Since its first creation, less than thirty years ago, the peerage has largely increased in numbers. The first list comprised 504 names. The present contains 923, all the new creations being those of men who have distinguished themselves in the military or civil service of the Government, or as scientists, bankers or merchants, and no bar of birth or descent has been permitted to interfere with the social advancement of those who eminently merited it. Many commoners of plebeian descent, whose fathers were little better than abject serfs, are now peers.

It was in 1884 that Ito returned from Europe. He was created a Count in the new peerage and nominated by the Emperor as the first Minister President under the new regime. Recurring complications with Korea and China were added to the domestic burthens of his office, but they did not prevent him from personally presiding over a commission which for the next five years was engaged in the framing of the new constitution. This task was completed and the constitution was promulgated in 1889 with impressive ceremonial and amidst universal national rejoicing, and in the following year the first Parliament that was ever seen in any Oriental state was duly elected and met.

The Parliament, or, to use its proper title, The Imperial Diet, consists of two Houses, a House of Peers of 300 members, who are partly hereditary, partly elective and partly nominated by the Emperor, and a House of Representatives, at first of 300 members but since increased to 379 members, elected for a maximum of four years on a high franchise. The House of Peers has always discharged with dignity its function of acting as a barrier against hasty or drastic reform and has never allowed any licence to tarnish its own proceedings, but it soon became evident that the lower House was to be made the instrument of a new and more persistent and violent agitation against the Government than that which had characterized the preceding two decades. The constitution was from the first a disappointment to those who had so strenuously fought for it. They had hoped to receive as their reward one founded on that of Great Britain. Instead of that they received one based on the model of Germany by which the cabinet is rendered independent of the Parliament and is responsible to and holds its office at the will of the Emperor alone. Considerable powers were at the same time conferred on the Parliament and great privileges secured to the people, but the predominant feature in the constitution is the precise reservation of Imperial prerogatives that can be used at any time to delay or nullify the legislation of the Parliament.

Numerous political parties had been founded during the antecedent decades of agitation, and when the House of Representatives first met no less than seven were represented among its members, all more or less antagonistic to each other, but all united in one common bond of opposition to the Government. Their object was to establish party government, with a ministry that must take its mandate from and owe its existence to their House, and the methods which they adopted to that end were those of rendering bureaucratic government impossible, of obstructing by every device that could be taken without distinct violation of the rules of the House all measures whether of finance or legislation that were brought before it by the Government.

The Government, on its part, showed no disposition to bend before either vituperation or obstruction. It, too, availed itself to the utmost of the principles of the constitution that were in its favour. Suspensions and dissolutions of the House were frequent. There were no less than three dissolutions in less than four years. One occurred after a single session lasting only eighteen days, but when bitterness was at its very worst and it almost seemed as if the government could not be carried on, war broke out with China. In a moment, everything was changed. Patriotism united the people, high and low, when they had to face a foreign foe. All domestic differences were forgotten and, while the war lasted, supplies were cheerfully voted and not a murmur of opposition was heard, even from the most violent agitators, against any measure that was taken by the Government in the national interests. Nor did this spirit entirely die after the war was over. Some of the parties no longer invariably ranged themselves alongside the extremists and the Government was, in some of its most important measures, supported by a majority of the House, while purely factious opposition was confined to a steadily decreasing minority. But by none of the parties was the old aim, though its vigorous expression was suppressed in some, ever abandoned and the story of the long struggle which they maintained is in many of its aspects not a pleasant one. Throughout it has been one rather of persons than of principles. It has at times been tainted with open and shameless corruption and votes were, it was known, freely sold and bought, while the Government on its side rewarded those who supported it with subordinate appointments or with honours.

It was not till 1900, after the House had been in existence for ten years, that a marked change occurred. Then Ito, who had been advanced to the dignity of a Marquis after the China war, the great Prime Minister, the creator of the constitution and of the Parliament, was induced to enter into the ranks of politicians and to become the head of a newly formed party which assumed the title of "Rikken Seiyukai," "Association of Friends of Constitutional Government," and the great influence and personal magnetism of its head soon enabled this party to obtain a commanding majority in the House. Its guiding principle is avowed to be not that of party government, for which the majority of its members had been strenuously fighting for ten years, but the conservation of the Imperial prerogative of nominating the ministry regardless of party while at the same time giving due consideration to the expressed will of the people. Some of its members entered the cabinet and from this time a political party became a distinct power in the executive. Its members gradually acquired a greater sense of their responsibility to the nation and sounder judgment in the exercise of their rights, and as they did so they gained more and more the confidence of the people whom they represented.

Among all parties the Seiyukai has retained the predominance which it acquired at its inception. Its founder and great leader has passed away, and has been succeeded by Marquis Saionji, the head of an old family of the Court nobility, a cadet branch of the Fujiwara, and as such the natural inheritor of the most ultra-conservative and aristocratic instincts. He had a comparatively long tenure of the Premiership, during the whole of which the Seiyukai was naturally the Government party, in close alliance with the elder statesmen (Genro) as they are called, the survivors of the great constructive statesmen and soldiers who took an active part in the Restoration and who created New Japan, as distinct from those who rose to eminence in later years. He again accepted the Premiership in 1912 when his party held a commanding majority in the House. But this time his tenure of office was short. The avowed policy of himself and his party was that of national economy and retrenchment in the public services. He was at once met with a demand by his own Minister of War for two additional divisions of the Army (a mobilised division consists of about 18,000 men) for service in Korea, and when this demand was rejected, with the full approval of the leading representatives of business and finance, the Minister resigned and

no one could be found to take his place. The terms
of the Constitution require that both the Ministers
of War and of the Navy shall be members of the services, and the Government was in fact boycotted by
all the senior officers of the army. The Premier,
though at the head of an overwhelming majority in
the House and confident of the approval of the
country, was helpless and had no choice but to
resign.

He was succeeded by Prince Katsura, who had
previously held the Premiership during some of the
most eventful years in Japan's modern history, the
years which witnessed the conclusion of the Anglo-
Japanese alliance, the triumphant war with Russia,
and an immense development of trade and industry,
but which also witnessed an equally immense increase
of national debt and taxation. Prince Katsura is
a distinguished soldier as well as a statesman and
an ex-samurai of the Choshiu clan, the members of
which have held a supremacy in the army ever since
its formation. He is also one of the elder statesmen,
and as such a champion of bureaucracy and an
inflexible opponent of any concession to party
government. It seemed therefore as if his return
to political leadership had secured a double triumph,
one for the old system of bureaucracy as against
political parties, and the other for the militarists,
consisting almost exclusively of men of Choshiu origin,

as against both their colleagues in the executive and the nation in general.

But Prince Katsura's tenure of the Premiership on this occasion was even shorter than that of his immediate predecessor and might be numbered by days rather than by months. A storm of opposition was aroused not only in the House but throughout the country. The Constitutionalists (Seiyukai) were firm and united and uncompromising in their determination to refuse all sanction to the proposals of the military party. They were not only of themselves in an overwhelming majority in the House, quite sufficiently so to be able to wreck any budget of which they disapproved, but were supported both by the sympathy and the active co-operation of members of other parties, and repeated suspensions of the session entirely failed to modify their attitude. Political mass meetings, held all over the country and attended by crowds, whose interest in politics had hitherto been dormant, enthusiastically endorsed what they had done and in not a few cases the meetings were followed by serious riots and by the mobbing of the few members of the House who were supporters of the Government. The bureaucratic Premier had to yield to the voice of the nation, and Prince Katsura resigned.

He has been succeeded by Admiral Yamamoto, who has had a long official career as Minister of the

Navy in many cabinets. He is not himself a member of the Seiyukai nor has he ever committed himself to any party in politics. But the members of his new cabinet are almost exclusively also members of the Seiyukai, and the cabinet may therefore be said to represent the principles of that party and its formation to herald the nearer approach of the time when the constitution will be interpreted or amended as they claim it should be. The Emperor will continue to be paramount but he must exercise his authority in accordance with the will of the nation as expressed by its chosen representatives and not solely by the advice of a small ring of statesmen of conservative prejudices, no matter how great their experience or how distinguished their past services. Prophecies are dangerous in any country, more so perhaps in Japan, where the unexpected has always happened, than in others, and they would be especially so if made as to the immediate future of domestic politics. Members of the Seiyukai were prominent in Ito's cabinet of 1900 and the party had then also a majority in the House. Then also it seemed as if the attainment of party government was within measurable view, but failure was the result and bureaucracy had a new lease of life. The political education of the people has, however, since made great progress, and the national apathy with which the first failure was received has changed into a vivid and almost universal excitement, which causes the problem of the future government of Japan to be one that is full of interest.

CHAPTER VI

RECOVERY OF NATIONAL AUTONOMY

THROUGHOUT the whole period during which the Government were struggling with their own people to resist the premature demand for parliamentary representation, they were at the same time engaged in a diplomatic struggle with Western Powers which taxed their ability, courage, and determination to no less a degree than did the first.

The system of extra-territorial jurisdiction was introduced into all the original Treaties concluded between the Government of the Shogun and the Western Powers. Under this system, foreigners residing in or visiting Japan were exempted from the jurisdiction of Japanese law and were answerable, both in civil and criminal matters, only to their own authorities, administering the laws of their own countries. The framers of the treaties in stipulating for it, only followed an invariable precedent in all intercourse between Western and Oriental nations, ever since the establishment of the Ottoman Empire at Constantinople, one which is still jealously guarded in the case of every non-Christian country in the world except Japan. Even without these precedents, it would have been impossible to contemplate the subjection of Europeans to the jurisdiction of a nation whose laws were unknown but who, it was known, practised torture, persecuted Christians, and recognised no rights of personal freedom or security. The Shogun's ministers, on their side, were entirely ignorant of all principles of international law and custom and, unconscious that they were placing their country on any lower level than those with which they were forming new relations, they willingly agreed to the surrender of their sovereign rights of judicial and tariff autonomy.

In the first decade which elapsed after the conclusion of the treaties, while the Shogunate was still in power, no attempt was made to alter the situation which was thus created. The internal condition of Japan and the complications with foreigners to which it gave rise were sufficient to absorb all the attention of the tottering Government without adding to its difficulties that of attempting to obtain any relaxation of the bonds that had been willingly signed. When the Emperor's Government came into office it had to assume all the obligations of these bonds and accept the situation which had been created by its predecessors. But, in the meantime, Japan had grown in knowledge and had learned both theoretically and by very bitter experience that the extra-territorial provisions of the treaties were a national stigma, derogatory to the prestige of a civilised and independent state.

The disabilities imposed on her by the treaties were sufficiently glaring to justify her utmost discontent. Identical treaties were made with no less than eighteen Western Powers, each one of which had its own system of consular jurisdiction and administered its own national laws, and only one among them all ever made provision for their full and effective administration. Great Britain, almost from the very first, established not only consular courts at every port at which foreigners were permitted to reside, presided over by highly-trained officers, qualified for the discharge of the important judicial duties that were entrusted to them and vested with very extensive powers of both civil and criminal jurisdiction, but founded a court of appeal in Japan and a still higher court at Shanghai, both of which exercised unlimited jurisdiction and were administered by judges whose professional ability and experience were unquestionable. The British Minister was also vested with legislative powers under the Sovereign's Orders in Council which enabled him at his discretion to give legal sanction, so as to make them enforceable in the local English courts, to any Japanese laws and ordinances that could equitably be applied to his countrymen.

The case was very different with all other Powers. No other ministers were vested with the law-making prerogative of their British colleague. None could render Japanese ordinances enforceable on their countrymen, who might therefore violate with impunity regulations, such as those of quarantine, which were essential for the general welfare of Japanese and foreigners alike. The consuls of most were trading consuls, quite incompetent to exercise judicial functions, not always honest in the exercise of such capacity as they possessed, and even *consuls de carrière* were very limited in the extent of the jurisdiction that was conferred on them by their own governments, so that capital and other serious offences committed by their countrymen generally went entirely unpunished. There were no courts of appeal nearer than Leipzig, Paris or Washington, which were entirely inaccessible to Japanese prosecutors or plaintiffs, and gross miscarriages of justice in serious cases, even when facts and law were entirely beyond dispute, were the rule rather than the exception.

Very early in its career the Emperor's Government attempted to procure a revision of the treaty clauses which they felt inflicted so great a wrong on their country. In 1871, a great embassy was sent to Europe for the purpose, but as was natural it totally

failed in its object. The laws and system of punishment in Japan, though greatly modified from what
they had been when the treaties were made, were
still founded on the old Chinese models and entirely
inapplicable to Europeans. Torture was still practised. Not only was the offensive prohibition of
Christianity still in public existence, but native
Christians were actually being cruelly persecuted at
the time when the Embassy was on its mission. The
chief result that ensued from it was the enforcement
of the lesson on Japan that there was no prospect of
the realisation of her desire until she reformed her
legal system and penal codes on European standards.

It is not an exaggeration to say that the recovery
of the full national rights with which she had parted
in her ignorance was the motive which mainly in-
spired all Japan's great reforms. It was that which
urged her to reform her legal system ; to withdraw
the prohibition of Christianity and make all religion
free ; to raise the material and educational status
of her people to the level of the most enlightened
nations of the West, so that their claim might become morally unanswerable ; and to develop her
great military system so that her claim, if refused
on moral grounds, might be backed by force.

Long years of wearisome diplomatic negotiations
passed away and Japan had given the most ample
evidence of her own advance in all the elements of

internal civilisation before her aspirations were at last realised. At first the negotiations were carried on in Tokio, where two conferences were held, the first in 1882 and the second in 1886, between the Minister for Foreign Affairs and the assembled Diplomatic Representatives of all the Treaty Powers. Under the treaties, foreigners enjoyed the rights to reside and trade only at certain cities on the coast, specified in the treaties and known as the open ports, and in Tokio; but from the middle of the seventies they had also been permitted as a privilege to travel in the interior for purposes of health or pleasure. This concession, it may be remarked, speedily became the source of very considerable gain to Japan from the money spent both by residents and travellers, which steadily increased with the development of travelling facilities and of the know-ledge of all the great natural beauties of the country. The opening up of the whole country to both trade and residence was offered in return for the abolition of•the objectionable clauses in the treaties, but even this concession, with all its possible commercial advantages, was not sufficient to overcome the re-luctance of Great Britain to submit her citizens to the jurisdiction of laws that were neither as yet tolerable in themselves nor furnished with complete machinery for their administration.

The difficulties which the Japanese negotiators

had to overcome were enough to dishearten the most optimistic among them. They had to deal with the representatives of eighteen Powers, all of whom were of equal rank, all with equal rights to a hearing, so that the British representative, with the duty of safe-guarding immense commercial and shipping interests and the persons and property of a large resident British population, surpassing at that time in both cases the aggregate of those of all other nationalities in Japan, had only the same voting power in the conferences as the representatives of Austria and Spain, who had neither trade nor citizens to protect, or of such insignificant Powers as Portugal and Belgium, whose captiousness was not infrequently in inverse ratio to their legitimate influence. All the treaties contained "most favoured nation" clauses which entitled all the Powers to claim any special concessions that were made to any one without sub-mitting to the conditions that accompanied them. All the Powers were supposed to be acting in har-mony, but their representatives had each different axes to grind. Russia's interests in Japan were entirely political and she cared nothing for trade nor for the protection of European residents in Japan among whom few of her own subjects were included. Great Britain carried on a great import trade and it was her object to prevent that trade from being burthened with oppressive duties. The

United States on the other hand, though the largest purchaser of Japan's exports, had then practically no import trade and were therefore able, without any cost to themselves, to give full indulgence to a sentimental friendship and their warmest support to Japan's claim to complete tariff autonomy. And similar differences were apparent in the cases of all the other great Powers, while as to the smaller, with no material interests whatsoever, without either moral influence or any pretence of military strength, it was within the prerogative of any one to render nugatory formal concessions even if they were unanimously made by all the others.

When further progress had been made in legal reform, Great Britain withdrew in some degree from the rigid attitude she had hitherto preserved, and in conjunction with Germany and the United States gave a modified acceptance to the Japanese proposals. But then a new difficulty arose. The political intelligence of the people had advanced in ratio with their material progress. The press had grown in influence and ability, and it was now openly declared by the people and in the press that no half measures could be tolerated and that no revision of the treaties could be accepted that was limited with conventional restrictions of any kind, or that failed to confer on Japan the fullest rights of an independent and civilised nation. A violent agitation spread throughout

the whole country and it was accompanied by a
dangerous outbreak of anti-foreign prejudice, one
incident in which was the attempted assassination of
the present Czar of Russia, who as Czarewitch was
then visiting Japan. An attempt was also made to
assassinate Count Okuma, at that time Minister for
Foreign Affairs, and when the first Parliament met
under the new constitution, its members were no less
persistent and outspoken than their constituents in
urging upon the Government its duty to obtain,
without further procrastination, the realisation of
the national aspirations in their widest sense.

Nearly twenty years had elapsed since Japan had
made her first essay towards procuring a revision
of the obnoxious Treaties and she seemed at this
juncture, notwithstanding all the evidence she had
given of material progress and of her desire to har-
monize her institutions with those of the West, to
be no nearer the end than she had been at first.
European residents in Japan of nearly all nationalities still contemplated with the strongest aversion
their unconditional subjection to the jurisdiction of
the native judicial and executive officials and were
strong enough to bring pressure that could not be
ignored to bear on their Diplomatic Representatives
on the spot. And the Japanese people were still
more adamant in their insistence that no revision
which was not entirely unconditional would solace

their long-outraged national dignity or be in keeping
with the terms of the constitution they had just
obtained. Then, when matters were at their very
worst and a hopeless impasse seemed to have been
reached, the Japanese Ministers gave one more proof
of the marked diplomatic talent which they had
already displayed on several occasions in international affairs and have since so frequently testified
both in war and peace.

They suddenly terminated all discussion in Tokio,
disregarded the representatives of the Powers with
whom they had so long been vainly arguing, and
transferred all their activities to Europe where they
dealt not with the Powers in conference but with
each separately and under the pledge of secrecy.
Great Britain was still the Power whose consent it
was most important to win, though she no longer
held the predominant moral, commercial or military
prestige in the Far East which she did throughout
the earlier negotiations. Both Germany and the
United States were now beginning to show themselves as commercial rivals and to display their
naval flags where they had been seldom seen before.
Sir Harry Parkes, the masterful minister of long
Eastern experience, had gone and had been followed
by successors who had neither experience nor knowledge of Japan, and whose last idea in their own
interests was to criticise or oppose any steps that

Sir Harry S. Parkes

might be taken by the Department at home under which they served and which would be the arbiter of their future careers. In the Foreign Office in London, the astute Japanese Minister accredited to Great Britain had an easy task. Its officials, both ignorant and badly advised as to the interests they were sacrificing, yielded to all his proposals and on July 18, 1894, a treaty was signed in London which unconditionally conceded everything that was necessary to realise the most extravagant Japanese claims. The other Powers gradually, though in some instances slowly and reluctantly, followed Great Britain's example, not however without securing as a *quid pro quo* some slight concessions for the benefit of their trade and countrymen in Japan to which the British Foreign Office had been loftily indifferent, and on June 30, 1899, the operation of all the old treaties came simultaneously to an end and for the first time in history, large, rich, and intelligent European communities became subject to the unfettered jurisdiction of an Oriental and non-Christian Power.

It was naturally a day of universal rejoicing throughout Japan, even more so than that of the promulgation of the constitution. The ambition persistently cherished and fought for throughout more than a quarter of a century had at last been attained and Japan had won her entry on terms of absolute equality into the comity of nations. European

L.   6

residents in Japan looked, however, to the future
with profound misgivings. They thought that their
personal liberty, hitherto securely guarded by their
own authorities, was endangered, that their trade
was threatened with ruin, and that their lives would
become intolerable under the petty persecutions to
which they would be always liable at the hands of
the lower classes of the Japanese officials. Their experience as plaintiffs or prosecutors in the Japanese
civil and criminal courts filled them with dismay
when they thought of what it would be when they
were forced to appear in the roles of defendants or
accused. Hitherto they had been immune from
taxation ; they would henceforth be liable to whatever burthens a parliament, in which they were
entirely unrepresented, whose members bore them
no goodwill, might impose on them. The feelings with which they contemplated the new order
of affairs to which they would thenceforward have
to bow their heads, may be aptly compared to those
of the most implacable Ulster Orangeman, when he
thinks of his future under Home Rule, with the
single exception that they anticipated none of the
interference with their religion on the part of heathen
governors of another race which the Orangeman
professes to dread from his Roman Catholic fellow-
countrymen. The voteless British residents in Japan
had no one to voice their grievances in Parliament,

and the new conditions, harsh though they seemed, had to be accepted. When that was recognised, all the European communities at once united as practical business men to make the best of what was irretrievable and they were aided in doing so by a new spirit which developed itself among the Japanese.

All lingering traces of the old anti-foreign prejudices seemed to disappear at once. That this was so was primarily due to the Emperor who issued a special rescript to his people, declaring :—

his earnest wish that all his subjects should unite with one heart to associate cordially with the people from far countries and that his officials of all classes should observe the utmost circumspection in the discharge of their duties, so that Japanese and Foreigners might enjoy equal privileges and advantages.

The Emperor's wishes are received by his subjects as divine commands, and as such they were now unreservedly obeyed. The instances in which Japanese officials have made arbitrary or unjust use of the powers with which they are now vested have been of rare occurrence, and few of the forebodings of the Europeans have been realised, natural as they were at the time. They have had to submit to regulations, many of which are inconsistent with their conceptions of personal freedom, to heavy personal taxation, to oppressive duties on their trade, and in some instances to inequitable decisions in the local courts of justice. But their trade, so far from being ruined, has more than doubled in its volume if not in its profits, and they have enjoyed a greater degree of personal liberty and of security of life and property than is accorded to foreigners in many Christian countries. Japan has not shown herself to be unworthy of the trust that has been reposed in her, hazardous as it was thought by the most competent authorities to be at the time at which it was conferred.

CHAPTER VII

TRADE AND INDUSTRY

IT was in 1858 that the first European traders began to take up their residences at Yokohama, then a mere fishing village but the nearest available port to the Shogun's capital, and that Japan became open to the commerce of the world.

The story of the beginning of her commercial intercourse is not a pleasant one to recall. The earliest foreign traders, like the Dutch at Desima during the years of Japan's seclusion, acquired very large profits principally owing to the differences in the relative values of gold and silver in Japan and in the rest of the world. In Japan the ratio was as one to four, and in the rest of the world one to fifteen, and a silver dollar obtainable for 4s. 6d. in China, distant only a few days' steaming, could in Japan be exchanged into a gold token that was worth over eighteen shillings in all the rest of the world. Trade conducted under such conditions was in itself sufficiently profitable to dazzle the most extreme optimism, but still greater profits were to be obtained from dealings in the currency itself without even a pretence of trade. Gold was exported in such quantities as to threaten the country with the denudation of its whole supply, and when the only possible remedy was taken in altering the relative values in Japan, all internal finance and economy were completely dislocated. Prices rose to a degree hitherto undreamt of, and the only persons to profit by the rise were the producers of silk, tea and vegetable wax, the only commodities to appear among Japan's original exports, while the rest of the people suffered intense distress.

Trade had always been despised, always regarded as the lowest in the scale of honour of all human vocations. It is not to be wondered at that their first modern experience of its conduct with the outward world should have tended not only to intensify the contempt previously felt for it by the Japanese, but to add hatred almost for its very name. It brought nothing to them that they wanted, except firearms, which were used during the succeeding years in slaughtering each other, while it enormously enhanced the cost of their own products that were in most general consumption.

Throughout the remaining years of the Shogunate, after the original difficulties of the currency had been overcome, trade continued to be hampered by vexatious difficulties and restrictions. That carried on with the Dutch had been always subject to the strictest Government control, and though the new treaties provided that it should be entirely free in this sense, old customs could not be eradicated in a day and it was still subject to constant official interference. The foreign merchants and the Japanese dealers were ignorant of each other's languages and customs, and of the values of what each had to sell. Both were full of mistrust, and, owing to the national odium which rested on all trade, only a very low class of Japanese, outcasts of their own people, without capital or sense of honour, at first entered upon that which was foreign. Their dishonesty and trickery brought upon their class an unsavoury reputation which still clings to their present-day representatives, some of whom, now millionaires, are the direct descendants of the early pioneers. On the other side, there were not wanting among the foreigners many who took advantage of their native clients' ignorance and inexperience to carry out transactions that could only be characterised as shameful frauds.

Notwithstanding all its difficulties, trade advanced even under the Shogunate, and in the first year of Meiji was estimated to have reached a value of about seven millions sterling. The Japanese had by this time learned to appreciate the quality and cheapness of English cottons and bought them largely, though firearms and old and obsolete steamers most appealed to them among all that Europeans could supply. The value of their exports was then very considerably in excess of that of the imports. During the sixties the silk husbandry of France and Italy was brought to the verge of ruin by an epidemic of pebrine plague in the silkworms. The worms died in multitudes, and the cocoons of those that survived furnished only a fraction of the normal quantity of silk. It was at this time that the raw silk of Japan became known in Europe, and its excellent quality immediately caused it to be in such demand that, in 1868, the value of its export was nearly three millions sterling. Japan might then have laid the foundation of a trade which would ultimately have given her the command of all the silk markets of the world. But French and Italian graineurs, while eager to buy her raw silk, were still more eager to buy the eggs of her healthy silkworms in order to replenish their own exhausted stock, and the prices which, during a few years, they were willing to pay for them tempted the native farmers, who were incapable of looking to the future, to devote themselves to the rearing of silk-worms for the sake of their eggs rather than to the production of silk. The best eggs were sold and exported to Europe, where by their means the plague-stricken industry was soon recuperated, while that in Japan, where only inferior eggs with diminished productive power had been left, for a time declined. The Japanese farmer had killed the geese which laid the golden eggs. When a healthy race of worms could again be reared in Europe, he found that there was no further demand for his eggs; his raw silk had lost much of its original excellence, and he had a long struggle before he was able to repair the damage which he suffered from his own short-sighted greed. Tea was the export that was next in value to silk and silkworm's eggs. Its peculiar flavour commended it to the American taste and, from the first, it found a market there which it retains to the present. These three staples represented nine-tenths of the whole export trade of the year. Some copper and vegetable wax were also exported, but the only articles to which the term "manufactures" could possibly be extended were curios of porcelain, bronze or lacquer ware, and their whole value did not exceed £50,000.

The Imperial Government was in its early years too absorbed in both domestic and foreign politics to be able to give much attention to the direct encouragement of trade and industry, and Japanese traders were too deficient in enterprise and self-reliance, to venture, unled and unaided, into new spheres except in the most timorous and tentative fashion. The national finances, too, were in a state of utter disorganisation. A mint, under the management of English experts of high standing, was founded and the coins which issued from it were unimpeachable in quality and appearance, but from 1869 onwards till 1881 the balance of foreign trade was steadily against Japan with the exception only of 1876, when exceptional circumstances for once turned it the other way. The coins issued from the mint went abroad to pay for the balance, and the only currency in domestic circulation was paper.

The new Government was, from the first, hampered by serious financial embarrassments. It succeeded to an empty treasury and while, in its early years, its expenditure was large, its revenue was collected slowly and with difficulty, and the only method that could be found of discharging its liabilities was by the issue of inconvertible paper notes. Recurring annual deficits in the budgets necessitated continuous increases in these issues, and an equally continuous depreciation in their exchange value for specie naturally followed, until the climax was reached shortly after the suppression of the Satsuma rebellion, the cost of which had been defrayed by a further large

issue of paper, when the inconvertible notes fell to
a discount of over 80 per cent. Specie continued to
flow out of the country. Within it, there was an
abnormal appreciation of prices and rates of interest,
and the most competent European authorities believed it was on the verge of national bankruptcy.
In such circumstances, the wonder is rather that
trade showed any increase at all—its value nearly
doubled in the period of twelve years—than that it
did not develop with the leaps and bounds that we
grew accustomed, in later years, to associate with
Japan's commercial progress. For the progress which
it did make at that time Japan is entirely indebted
to the resident European merchants, among whom
those of British nationality were far predominant,
whose honesty, capacity and enterprise remedied,
vis-à-vis buyers and consumers in Europe, the de-
ficiencies that were universally characteristic of the
native traders. In 1882, the Government woke up
to the necessity of drastic financial reform. European
expert advisers had suggested various remedies, including foreign loans and national lotteries. But
a foreign loan could only have been obtained at very
high interest and some reliable item of the revenue
must have been earmarked to meet it, while gam-
bling, in any shape or form, has in all ages been
forbidden by Japanese law. The Government had
to rely on its own efforts to get Japan out of the

financial morass into which she had been driven by her early necessities.

Sweeping economies were effected in the public expenditure and simultaneously a substantial increase was made in taxation. Industrial and agricultural undertakings which had been established during the preceding decade, with the double purpose of affording educational models to the people and bringing some revenue to the Government, were sold. By these means a large surplus was obtained in the annual budget which was applied to the redemption of the paper currency in circulation. Then the Government itself practically became a trader. Two Banks were established under its auspices, the Bank of Japan, to act as the agent of the Government in its domestic finances, and the Yokohama Specie Bank, to serve in a similar capacity in its foreign financial affairs. Native produce was bought through the first and paid for with paper and sold abroad through the second for specie which was collected and stored in the Treasury. The balance of trade now turned in favour of Japan, and during the three years 1882—1884 there was a surplus of exports over imports of more than 20 million yen, so that the Government measures were considerably facilitated. Their result was that soon after the close of the year last mentioned, the paper currency in circulation was reduced by 80 million yen, and the Government

had at its disposal a specie reserve of 42 million
yen. Confidence was restored. The currency, which,
in 1882, was at a discount of eighty per cent. was
early in 1885 almost at par, and in the autumn of
the same year the Government was able to announce,
that the hitherto purely fiduciary paper would be
exchanged at the Bank of Japan for its face value
in specie.

It was in 1885 that Japan, in the confidence
engendered by the restoration of her financial stability, began to furnish omens of her coming commercial and industrial progress. The value of her
foreign trade in 1874, when her customs service had
been thoroughly organised and its statistics had
become unimpeachable, was 42 million yen. In 1884,
the value had only grown to 53 million yen. Ten
years later it was 230 million yen, and in yet another
decade (1904) it had reached 690 million yen. Its
movement was still onwards, and in 1912 its value
amounted to 1145 million yen. The population of
the Empire also largely increased. In 1884, it was
37½ million, and in 1912 it was estimated at 52¼
million, exclusive of Formosa and Korea. In 1884,
the ratio of the value of her foreign trade to the
population was 1·67 yen per head ; in 1894, 5·52 yen ;
in 1904, 14·63 yen, and in 1911, 18·65 yen.

In 1884, Japan's exports were still confined to
agricultural, mining and marine products—silk, tea,

coal, copper and dried fish. The only manufactured
articles included amongst them, to any substantial
extent, were matches, an industry acquired from the
West, and such indigenous products as porcelain,
lacquer and bronze ware, and plaited straw ware.
The cotton spinning industry had been initiated and
raw cotton was imported for its requirements, but
with that exception almost all the imports were highly
finished manufactures. It was already recognised,
however, by her statesmen that her future industrial
prosperity depended rather on the development of
her manufacturing than of her agricultural industry.
The capacity of the latter had its limits, and while it
would no doubt remain, as it had always been, the
greatest of all national industries, there was no hope,
even with the intensive system of culture that was
universally followed throughout the whole country, of
its being able to provide for the future support of
a population increasing with such rapidity as was
that of Japan, where it was foreseen that the time
was within measurable view when 100 million people
would have to be supported, and that too in a land
which in the past had on many occasions in years of
dearth been unable to provide the absolute necessaries of life for less than a third of that number.
The intelligence, docility and deftness, which the
people possessed in an eminent degree, must be
directed into new channels of industrial skill and

activity, and Japan made in the progress of time the workshop of the Far East, just as Great Britain was of the West.

Every natural advantage existed to aid in the attainment of this end. Japan not only possessed, like Great Britain, an ample supply of coal, but had also at her disposal what Great Britain had not, an immense water-power in her lakes at high altitudes and her rapidly-flowing rivers. Her coasts were everywhere indented by capacious harbours, and close to her was the great Empire of China, with whose people she had many common ties, whose tastes and requirements she had opportunities and means of studying that were wholly lacking in European competitors for her great markets. To acquire a control, in the first instance, of the foreign trade of China and subsequently to extend her commercial activity even as far as India was an ambition that presented itself to Japanese statesmen as one that was not beyond the capacity of their people to realise in the process of time.

No measure that could train and stimulate the people to that end was neglected. A department of Agriculture and Commerce was organised in the Government and the best officials and experts were employed in it. Commercial and technical training schools were established throughout the Empire. Liberal subsidies were granted to infant industries, and the press and the platform were freely used both for teaching and encouragement. Banks, both for general and specific business, were founded so that credit facilities at moderate interest could be obtained, and they have had careers of almost unbroken success. The two great wars in which Japan was engaged and the Anglo-Japanese alliance had each their effect in promoting commercial prosperity. The indemnity that was obtained from the war with China was in part used to foster commercial activity and to establish her currency, hitherto of silver, on a gold standard. The enhanced national prestige which she acquired as the result of the war with Russia and of the alliance with Great Britain enabled her to become a borrower on moderate terms in the money markets of Europe, so that the heavy burthen thrown upon the nation by the cost of the war with Russia was met without a particle of financial disorganisation or distress.

One great obstacle to ultimate success was the insufficiency of internal transport facilities. This was overcome by the steady advance of railway construction until every district in the country was within easy reach of a line, and it became possible to travel from the extreme north to the extreme south of the Empire without leaving a station, except to cross the straits that separate Hokkaido, the northern, from Hondo, the main island, and Hondo from

Kiusiu. It was in 1873 that the first railway was opened to the public, a line of less than 20 miles between Yokohama and Tokio. In 1911, there were no less than 5355 miles in operation, all the property of the state. A great mercantile marine was also fostered by large subsidies both for the construction and navigation of ocean-going steamers of the highest class, not only for service in Eastern waters, but to carry the mercantile flag to the west coast of America, to India, Australia and England, and liners, managed with no less efficiency than those of the best known steamship companies of Great Britain, now regularly ply between the ports of those countries and of Japan and successfully carry on a large passenger and cargo trade.

The people have responded to the efforts of their Government. From the time that they could rely on the stability of their currency, they have shown a spirit of enterprise that was previously, with every reason that was founded on experience, believed to be entirely wanting in them. Numerous joint-stock companies for industrial purposes have been founded with ample capital, and have contributed much to the development of the spinning, weaving, engineering and ship-building industries. The working classes, among whom, as in England, there has been a large influx from the country to the towns, have adapted themselves to the new conditions of organised labour in large establishments,—all industry in Japan in former days was entirely domestic, carried on in a small way in separate households by members of the same family—and the descendants of the samurai, whose fathers despised the very name of trade and thought the smallest association with it contamination, now eagerly seek for employment in banks, in merchant houses and in factories, where they often serve under the orders of and are paid by commoners, whom their fathers would scarcely have deigned to admit to their presence, and where their higher ideals of probity in some degree remedy the lack of integrity which is still a prominent characteristic among those who have been born into the manufacturing and commercial classes.

Japan, which forty years ago could in one year only send abroad manufactured goods in the shape of a few *articles de luxe* to the value of less than £50,000, exported in eleven months of the year 1912, partly manufactured goods to the value of 23½ millions sterling and wholly manufactured to the value of 14¼ millions. They included cotton yarn, cotton and silk piece goods and handkerchiefs, clothing, umbrellas, matches, refined sugar, paper, floor matting, carpets, straw plaiting and cigarettes, and, to a minor extent, machinery, electric fittings, stoves, bicycles, boots, saddlery, trunks, cement, soap, tooth powder and brushes, chemicals, beer, mineral waters, clocks, lamps, stationery, glass ware and a hundred other miscellaneous articles, all of which she has learned to make from Europe and all of which find a ready market in China and in the Straits Settlements, where they are sold at prices with which even German makers cannot compete. The import of raw material and of machinery has kept pace with the development of manufacturing industry, and though a heavy protective tariff has now replaced the conventional tariffs of her early days of commercial intercourse with foreign countries, under which only an average *ad valorem* duty of 5 per cent. was levied on all imports, she bought over twenty million pounds worth of goods from Europe in 1912, nine-tenths of which may be said to have been fully manufactured. Great Britain no longer enjoys her former monopoly of this trade, but the value of British products is still two-fold that of the products of Germany, her greatest competitor, and if the purchases that Japan makes from the overseas dominions are added to those made from the parent country, the import trade of the British Empire to Japan represents more than 40 per cent. of the whole trade.

The present industrial position of Japan is, however, not all *couleur de rose* nor is its future so well defined as to place the realisation of the hopes of its founders beyond the realms of doubt. One of her early advantages was the abundance of cheap and

docile labour that was at her command. Labour is
no longer either so cheap or so contented to take
what it is offered as it was. The standards of life
have risen and what the fathers of the present
workmen regarded as luxuries are now demanded by
their sons as common necessaries. Wages have, in
thirty years, increased three-fold, and if the relative
productive capacity of the Japanese workman is fairly
compared with that of his English confrère, it may
be doubted if there is now a very marked difference
between the cost of labour in Japan and in England.
It is still cheaper, probably less than half, but its
quality is still far inferior and in factories the
aggregate of employees is still fully three-fold of
what would be considered necessary for the same
work in England. The old docility is no longer
a conspicuous element among the working classes.
They are still unorganised and have no trades unions
or combinations for the protection and advancement
of their class interests, but the men have learned
something of the rights of labour, and the craven
humility which feudal oppression engendered in them
has been replaced to no small extent by truculent
and offensive aggressiveness and by an intolerance of
any discipline other than that of the drill sergeant
during the period of military service. No ideas of
personal loyalty now bind them to their employers,
and socialism is not without its apostles though as

yet it has found few disciples. Wages have risen, but the cost of living following on more requirements, far higher prices even of the necessaries of life, and a heavy burthen of imperial and local taxation, has done so to a still greater degree. Workmen in Japan have not yet votes and have therefore no political influence. The benevolence of the legislature has as yet failed to benefit them either by factory acts regulating their hours of labour, or by Insurance or Compensation acts, and while feeling themselves the increasing strain of the struggle for life, they see very substantial dividends regularly paid by the companies they serve to rich and comfortable share-holders. The spirit already present and growing in them is not such as will induce them to submit indefinitely to this condition of affairs and the day may not be very far distant when the conflict between capital, though supported by a sympathetic legisla-ture, and labour, though politically powerless, may assume some of the aspects which it already presents in Europe.

CHAPTER VIII

FOREIGN RELATIONS. 1867—1895

IF the questions of Treaty Revision and Trade are excluded, Japan's Foreign Relations, from the Restoration down to the close of the Russian War,

may be said to have been confined to her three
nearest neighbours, China, Russia and Korea, and
the last named was the pivot on which the most
important controversies depended which she had
with the other two.

From the dark ages in which Japan, under the
leadership of her mythical Empress Jingo, claimed to
have conquered Korea, the latter acknowledged the
suzerainty of her conqueror in the usual Oriental
fashion by the payment of annual tribute. The
custom was at no period observed with absolute
regularity and it fell into total abeyance in the
anarchy that prevailed throughout Japan during the
long civil wars of the middle ages, but it was revived
at the beginning of the seventeenth century subsequent to Korea's second invasion and conquest by
Hideyoshi, the great military dictator of Japan, and
it thenceforward continued to be regularly observed
throughout the whole of the Tokugawa regime.
"Payment of tribute," it may be mentioned, was only
in form. It did not involve the transfer of any sums
of money, and was signified by the despatch of a
mission to the superior Power bearing certain specified
offerings of no great value. On the occasions of
Lord Macartney's mission to China in 1793 and of
Lord Amherst's in 1816 as ambassadors of George III,
the usual complimentary presents which they offered
to the Emperor were described in the Chinese official

gazette as "tribute," and the ambassadors themselves as tribute bearers to a superior Power.

Throughout all time, Korea, while thus outwardly acknowledging herself as a tributary of Japan, also not only admitted herself but claimed to be the vassal of China, to which she was bound by ties of gratitude, reverence and propinquity which had no existence in her relations with Japan. So far from that, the memories of all the sufferings she had undergone during Hideyoshi's ruthless invasion and of the national ruin which followed it, made the very name of Japan an object of bitter hatred to all her people, high and low. Korea also conserved her national isolation, even more rigidly than Japan had done prior to Perry's arrival. Her sole connections with the outward world were with Japan and China and all attempts by Europeans to enter the country were repulsed. The few French missionaries, who secretly made their way there, and all their converts were cruelly tortured and killed, and even the use of European goods was forbidden under pain of death. So conservative were the court and officials that they adhered to the dress and customs which they had adopted from China when under the Ming dynasty (1368—1644) and made no change in them throughout all the succeeding years in which they professed to be the obedient vassals of the Manchu Emperors.

After the Restoration, Japan sent letters to the

Korean Court informing it of the change of government. The letters were answered with contemptuous insult and the overtures of friendship which they contained were haughtily rejected. When, in 1873, this fact became public in Japan, the whole nation was in a ferment of indignation and angrily demanded that war should at once be declared. War with Korea would, however, almost certainly have ultimately involved war also with China, a task for which Japan was quite unfitted, and the Emperor, young as he then was, showed his wisdom and prudence by supporting the members of his ministry who had the courage to resist both the national outcry and their own colleagues in sympathy with it. Then occurred the first split in the Ministry, involving the resignations among other ministers of Itagaki and Saigo, but peace was preserved and the country permitted to continue without foreign complication in its great tasks of domestic reform and reorganisation.

Japan was, however, only biding her time. She did not forget Korea's insult. She also fully recognised the danger to her own territorial integrity, perhaps even to her continued independent existence, if Russia, then in her full career of Asiatic expansion, took possession of Korea, whose north-eastern boundaries were already conterminous with those of Russia's Far Eastern province of Primorski on the Pacific littoral. Korea, in her national ignorance and debility, consequent on her long seclusion from the outer world, could make no resistance against a great European military Power, while the magnificent ice-free harbours on her southern coast provided a bait for Russia that would in time prove irresistible. Japan resolved to take upon herself the mission, which the United States had accomplished in her own case, of dragging Korea out of her isolation, hoping thereby both to bring her into the sphere of international intercourse and to induce her to shake off the fetters of her effete Chinese civilisation and educate herself in Western science, as Japan was doing. Korea's immunity from foreign aggression might then be secured.

In 1875, a Korean fort fired on a Japanese gunboat which was surveying the mouth of the River Han, the river on which the capital lies about 20 miles from its mouth. It was a very insignificant occurrence, the action of a subordinate and ignorant officer, and it might be said to have been provoked by the gunboat, which was in Korean waters, access to which on the part of any foreign vessel for any reason was forbidden by Korean law. The most ample punishment for it was inflicted at the time, the gunboat having first shelled the fort and a landing party, against which the Koreans, armed only with bows and arrows and old matchlocks, could offer no effective resistance, having completed its destruction and

slaughtered the entire garrison. But the insult to
the flag provoked a new ferment in Japan and once
more war was demanded by hot-headed patriots.
There was no division in the Government on this
occasion. They were unanimous in taking a more
sober view than some of their predecessors had done
in 1873 and they were for once supported by the
press. War was not declared but an armed expedi-
tion was sent to Korea early in the following year.
Its object was peaceful, to induce Korea to enter into
a treaty of friendship, but following Perry's example
in Japan, it was quite prepared to use force if its
peaceful overtures failed.

The Koreans yielded and the treaty was signed
on February 26, 1876, the first step being thus taken
to end Korea's isolation. The provisions of the
treaty were in almost every detail precisely similar
to those in the treaties which Japan had herself,
when ignorant of international law and custom,
originally concluded with Western Powers and which
she afterwards so bitterly resented as a stain on her
national dignity. As the Western Powers had done
with herself, so did she now, without one particle of
compunction, induce Korea to sign away her sovereign
rights of executive and tariff autonomy and to confer
on Japanese residents within her borders all the extra-
territorial privileges which were held to violate equity
and justice when exercised by Europeans in Japan.

The history of Japan in the early days of her foreign intercourse was repeated with strange similarity in that of Korea, where Japan played the part that in her own case had been performed by the Western Powers. As in Japan, in those days, so in Korea, the nation was divided into two factions. One was saturated with conservative bigotry, and claimed that the old traditions of national isolation should, notwithstanding the treaty, be restored and maintained in their integrity. The other, less numerous and less influential in rank and reputation, influenced by what had been seen of the material progress which Japan had already made after twenty years of foreign intercourse, urged that Korea should follow Japan's example and endeavour like her to assimilate Western civilisation. In the capital, Seoul, the conservative faction was all-powerful and the people, cherishing the hatred of the Japanese that was transmitted to them from their fathers, were easily aroused. Just as the British Legation in Yedo was twice attacked by Japanese fanatics in the early sixties, so twenty years later was the Japanese Legation in Seoul twice attacked by infuriated mobs, with the same object of murdering all its inmates. On both occasions in Seoul, the inmates were able to fight their way out of the city and escape to the coast, but the Legation buildings were utterly destroyed. After both, the Koreans were forced to pay heavy indemnities and

to make national apologies, as were the Japanese by
the British Government, after the assaults in Yedo.
And just as the British and French established
garrisons of their own troops in Japan, so Japan after
the first outrage stationed a contingent of troops in
Korea.   Her action was even more humiliating to
Korea than that of the Western Powers to herself.
Their troops were quartered in Yokohama, twenty
miles from the capital, which they never entered.
Those of Japan in Korea were posted in the heart
of the capital, almost in the shadow of the King's
palace.

Japan in the treaty recognised Korea as "an independent state, enjoying the same sovereign rights"
as herself, and Korea by assuming this status theoretically terminated her vassalage to China. Similar
provisions were inserted in all Korea's later treaties
with Western Powers, including Great Britain, in all
of which Korea was dealt with as "an independent
nation free in her foreign relations from all control
by China."   But the ties between the great Empire
and "The Hermit Kingdom" were too close and of
too long duration to be ended by a stroke of the pen.
China showed no inclination to part with her old
tutelage, Korea equally little to cease to rely on her
suzerain for both protection and advice.   Li Hung
Chang, the great Viceroy, was at this time the
director of China's foreign policy.   He had neither

fear of nor respect for Japan and he was determined
that the interests of his own country in Korea should
not be those of sentiment only. His ablest and most
trusted lieutenant, Yuan Shi Kwai, who has since
become the first President of the Chinese Republic,
was sent to Korea early in the eighties as Resident-
General, and there during the next ten years he was
the *de facto* ruler of the country. The Japanese were
all this time urging reform on the Korean Government, but all their efforts were rendered nugatory by
the paralysing interference of Yuan Shi Kwai, and
by the administrative incompetence and gross corruption of the native officials. At the end of the
ten years, Korea had made no progress in the path
which had been marked out for her by the Japanese
at the beginning of their modern relations. She was
still incapable of defending herself against foreign
aggression. Her Government retained all its worst
vices ; the people sunk in abject and hopeless poverty,
spiritlessly cowering under official tyranny, indolent,
and thriftless, were the most wretched in the world,
as wretched under their own authorities as were the
Irish in the darkest periods of British maladministration, or the Bulgars when enduring the utmost
cruelties of Ottoman oppression.

In 1894, the people of southern Korea, maddened
by suffering, rose in rebellion with the avowed object
of removing from the side of their King " the corrupt

ministers and officials who were indifferent to the
welfare of the country." The ill-equipped and half-
hearted soldiers who were sent to quell the rebels were
repeatedly defeated and the Government, thoroughly
alarmed at the result of its own tyranny and incapacity, appealed to Yuan Shi Kwai for help. China
and Japan had covenanted in a treaty, defining their
respective positions in Korea, that neither should
send troops there without notice in advance to the
other. At this time domestic politics in Japan were
at one of their worst stages. The parliament was in
the full career of obstruction that marked the early
years of its existence and Li Hung Chang had been
advised by the Chinese minister in Tokio that Japan,
divided into bitterly antagonistic factions, was so
fully occupied with her own internal affairs, that she
could spare neither thought nor action for whatever
occurred abroad. As it proved, the minister completely misjudged the spirit of the nation, but at the
time it seemed that China could do as she pleased in
Korea without fear of further complication, and Li
Hung Chang, relying on the disastrous advice that
was given to him, decided to revive the old obligations of a suzerain and assume the task of restoring
order in the vassal kingdom. A force of 3000 troops,
all well drilled and armed, was sent from Tientsin
and landed at Asan, a port on the Korean coast
within striking distance of the headquarters of the

rebels. Formal notice of this step was given to Japan and she promptly replied by sending a force of 8000 men, complete in every detail of cavalry, artillery and infantry, which instead of remaining on the coast, as did the Chinese, at once entered the capital.

Some diplomatic negotiations ensued. Japan proposed that the reform of Korea should be jointly undertaken by herself and China. The proposal was flatly refused, whereupon Japan laid before the Korean Government an independent programme of reform and demanded its unqualified acceptance. Korea, encouraged by Yuan Shi Kwai, refused to discuss this programme so long as a Japanese army was in her capital, and when friction was at its height, an incident that might almost be called an accident occurred on the seas which rendered war inevitable. Li Hung Chang determined to reinforce his troops in Korea, and for that purpose chartered the "Kowshing," a British steamer, to transport 1500 men from Tientsin. When she was on her voyage, under the British flag, manned by British officers and a crew who, though of Chinese race, were British subjects, she was intercepted by the Japanese cruiser "Naniwa" under the command of the officer, then a post captain, who has since become world-famous as Admiral Togo and called upon to surrender and follow the "Naniwa" to a Japanese

port. The Chinese officers of the troops on board
forcibly prevented the master from complying with
this demand : a signal was made from the "Naniwa"
for Europeans to save themselves by jumping over-
board, a torpedo was discharged, and in a moment
the "Kowshing" was sinking. The master and some
of his deck officers saved themselves by swimming
until they were picked up by the "Naniwa's" boats,
but everyone else on board, most of the engine-room
staff of British engineers, the crew of British subjects,
and all the Chinese soldiers perished, the boats re-
fusing to save a single soul of Chinese race.

This occurred on the 25th of July 1894 and seven
days later war was formally declared by both Powers.
Two battles were fought on Korean soil and a naval
engagement took place in Korean waters off the
mouth of the Yalu river. Then, Japan having secured the command of the sea, the scene of the war
was transferred to Manchuria, where a campaign
ensued which lasted for six months. The perfection
of Japanese military organisation, which had provided every requisite that human foresight could
suggest for a winter campaign amidst the Arctic
rigours of the Manchurian mountains, and the bravery
of her officers and soldiers were equally manifested,
and victory, unbroken by a single reverse, though
tarnished on some occasions by cruel excesses, attended her arms both by sea and land throughout

the whole war. The great fortress of Port Arthur, its approaches both from land and sea guarded by heavily armed forts that had been constructed at great expense by European engineers according to the most modern principles of military science, was taken by storm, and the victorious army was on the high road to Peking, when China, beaten to her knees, made overtures for peace. Li Hung Chang had to swallow the bitter pill of proceeding to Japan, and after discussions which lasted nearly a month, a treaty of peace was signed at Shimonoseki on April 17, 1895. Assassination has, it has been mentioned before, been a recurring incident in all Japanese politics both ancient and modern. It was not wanting in the peace negotiations. While they were in progress an attempt to assassinate Li Hung Chang was made by a Japanese fanatic indignant at the thought that peace prevented the crowning triumph of the military occupation of Peking. That the old samurai spirit of Japan was not yet dead was manifested by the fact that fully a score of officers with the army in the field committed suicide in the orthodox method of *hara-kiri* for the same reason.

The principal terms of the treaty of peace provided that the Liao Tung peninsula, at the southern extremity of which lies the fortress of Port Arthur, and Formosa, together with the Pescadore islands which are adjacent to it, should be ceded to Japan ;

that a war indemnity of 200,000,000 taels should be
paid to her in eight instalments ; that Wei Hai Wei,
another fortified harbour, directly facing Port Arthur,
which had also been taken in the war, should be held
by her until the last instalment of the indemnity was
paid; and that China should for ever forego all claims
to suzerainty over Korea. Some valuable commercial
privileges were also secured, in the benefits of which
all Western Powers shared equally with Japan under
the most favoured nation clauses in their treaties.

Japan's triumph seemed to be complete. Her
diplomatists had been no less successful than her
generals and admirals. Her losses in life during the
war had been insignificant and the monetary cost
was recouped two-fold by the indemnity. She had
impressed all the world by her military capacity.
She had obtained a large accession of territory of
great strategic importance and of equally great po-
tential commercial value ; and above all she had
attained, in the fullest extent, the ostensible object
for which she fought and had finally ousted China from
Korea, where thenceforward she could anticipate a
free hand in whatever measures she might see fit to
adopt, either for the regeneration of Korea or the
promotion of her own material interests. But her
triumph was soon impaired by a blow as unexpected
as it was crushing.

Hardly had the ratifications been exchanged in

less than a month after the signing of the treaty, when, one morning, the chief diplomatic representatives in Tokio of Russia, France and Germany called without notice on the Minister for Foreign Affairs and presented to him a joint note in which Japan was advised, in the interests of the permanent peace of the East, to forego the cession of any Chinese territory on the mainland. The note contained no threats, but it was verbally intimated, in terms which left no doubt, that the three Powers were prepared if necessary to enforce the acceptance of their advice.

Japan was exhausted by the war: her military stores and money had been all used; her ships were in urgent need of extensive repairs; and her military authorities declared that she was incapable of resisting the new coalition which faced her. The national pride was bitterly wounded, but once more the Emperor took upon himself the responsibility of impressing on his people the necessity of accepting what was inevitable. None but he could have succeeded. In his rescript, he declared that:—

he had taken up arms for no other reason than his desire to secure for the Orient a lasting peace, that the friendly recommendations of the three Powers were equally prompted by the same desire, and that he therefore did not hesitate to accept them as in no way impairing the honour and dignity of his Empire.

The peninsula was restored to China, Japan receiving as a solatium an additional indemnity of

30,000,000 taels. She asked for a pledge that no portion of the retroceded territory should ever be given to any foreign Power, but it was categorically refused, and from that day she saw that war with Russia was inevitable in the future and she began to prepare herself so that when the time came she could enter on it with no less confidence in its result than that which had animated her when she flung down the gauntlet to China.

In the meantime she quickly testified her intention of honourably endeavouring to accomplish the aims which were the avowed object of the war. Her troops were withdrawn from both Korea and Manchuria as rapidly as transport could be found for them, and the reform of Korea, the task of leading or driving her into the path of progress, was entrusted to the veteran statesman, Count Inouye, who took up his new post as Minister at the Court of Seoul without delay. He had, as a cabinet minister, been long and closely associated with Sir Harry Parkes. No one knew better the share which Sir Harry Parkes had in the reform of Japan and he had now before him the rôle in Korea which Sir Harry Parkes had so successfully performed in Japan.

As one of the elder statesmen (Genro), Count Inouye held a position that was only second to that of Marquis Ito in the estimation of his countrymen. He was, like Ito, a Choshiu clansman, and was, like him, one of the earliest of the clansmen to be converted to the policy of opening the country and adopting Western civilisation. When five youths of the clan, braving the penalty of death or of life-long banishment, secretly left their country in May 1863, in order to study in England, Ito and Inouye were of their number, but while their companions made their journey from Shanghai to England in a mail steamer, Ito and Inouye shipped in a sailing ship and both worked their passages as ordinary seamen on the long voyage round the Cape, sharing throughout it the same food, accommodation and work as the rest of the crew. This they did in order to learn navigation, a knowledge of which they thought was a primary essential to Japan's material development. They had been in England only one year, during which they acquired a sound knowledge of the English language which neither ever lost in after life, when they heard of the complications between their feudal lord and the Western Powers which eventuated in the bombardment of Shimonoseki. They knew that the anti-foreign policy of Japan could only bring disaster, and both abandoned their studies and hastily returned home in order to stop their lord's folly even at the sacrifice of their lives, which were liable to legal forfeiture for having secretly left their country. Their efforts were in vain and the bombardment of Shimonoseki took place. Both nearly met their deaths

Ito   Inouye (Viscount)   Endo

Inouye (Marquis)   Yamao
The five Choshiu Students in England 1864

at the hands of their fellow-clansmen, who regarded them as traitors to their clan and to their country, and Inouye, who is happily still alive, bears many scars of the terrible wounds he received at the time. Both afterwards took an active share in all the struggles of the Restoration, and when it was accomplished both became subordinate officials of the new Government to which their knowledge of Western affairs and of the English language, then a very rare accomplishment, was of inestimable value. The rise of both was rapid. Ito, as already stated, became Minister President within sixteen years from the Restoration. Inouye filled many high offices in the Cabinet, including that of Minister for Foreign Affairs, and always showed himself to be possessed of a high degree of courage, firmness and tact, as well as of the fertility of resource, and the foresight and administrative ability that are essential in a great statesman. It was to this Minister that the Emperor entrusted the task which Japan had set herself in Korea.

The difficulties which confronted Inouye on his arrival were very great. China had been driven out of the peninsula and her active influence on its affairs eradicated, but the spirit of Chinese conservatism remained, and it found its exponent in the Queen, a woman of strong and vigorous character, scarcely less so than Tsu Hsi, the great Dowager Empress of China. She completely dominated her weak and vacillating husband, and was herself an inflexible opponent of reform and progress, and a champion of the venality and tyranny that had hitherto been the chief characteristics of the Court and Government. From the first Inouye found in her an effective barrier to the most important of his measures, and he was scarcely less handicapped by the conduct of his own countrymen in Korea. The worst rogues and bullies of Japan—and Japan produces abundance of both types—poured into the unfortunate country, and robbed and browbeat the terrified natives in a way that filled European witnesses with indignation and horror, and increased tenfold the traditional hatred of the natives to the very name of Japan. And Inouye himself made the one serious error in judgment that is apparent in the long record of his great career. He estimated the assimilative capacity of the Koreans by that of his own countrymen, and just as the latter were in 1871, apparently in a moment, converted from disciples of conservative bigotry into apostles of wholesale reform, so he thought could be the Koreans. He forgot that his great British proto-type in Japan had spent five years of earnest propagandism before Japanese statesmen were induced to enter whole-heartedly on the paths into which he was now anxious to lead the Koreans.

He succeeded in reorganising the military system and the local administration. But a host of other

reforms, which descended from national legislation
and finance down to the smallest details of domestic
life, bewildering to a people whose customs had
remained unchanged through centuries, could only
be kept alive by his own commanding influence.
When, after a year, he left Korea and was replaced
by a successor, who, though a Lieutenant-General in
the army and a Viscount in the peerage, proved to
be lacking in every quality of constructive and administrative statesmanship, all that he had done was
quickly undone and all the worst features of Korean
maladministration revived. Then occurred the most
shocking incident of the reign of the Emperor, one
that for its atrocity and cruelty in our own time
finds its only parallel in the murders of the King and
Queen of Servia. Viscount Miura, the new Japanese
Minister, saw in the Queen the principal obstacle to
the success of Japan's policy. She was hated by a
faction of the upper classes of her own people, who
knew that her influence would exclude them from all
share in the Government. Miura, equally forgetful
of the civilisation which his country claimed to have
acquired, of the mission which he had undertaken as
the apostle of order and legality, of the dignity of his
office, and of his own reputation, entered into a conspiracy with the leader of the Korean faction for the
murder of the Queen, and the object of the conspiracy
was accomplished during the night of October 7, 1895.

A mixed band of Koreans and Japanese, the latter including not only police and military officers, but even some members of the staff of Miura's Legation, surprised and overpowered the palace guards and, having made their way into the royal apartments, "slashed to death" the Queen and many of the ladies and officials of her court who tried in vain to hide or protect her. The corpses were saturated with paraffin and burnt in the courtyard.

When the incident, with its details of revolting cruelty, became known in Tokio, Miura and all his satellites were at once recalled and brought to trial, but all escaped through legal technicalities and suffered no other punishment than the dismissal of those who were in Government service. But even if they had paid the penalty of their savagery with their lives, the mischief they had done could not have been undone. Japan, at one blow, lost all the influence in Korea which her success in the war with China had won for her, and it was not regained until she had fought another and a greater war.

CHAPTER IX

FOREIGN RELATIONS. 1895—1913

IN 1884, Russia concluded a commercial treaty with Korea, and from that time was represented in Seoul by one of the ablest members of her diplomatic service. So long as China's influence was predominant, and afterwards during the regime of Count Inouye, he was content to play an unobtrusive part in local politics, but the murder of the Queen gave him a new opportunity. The terrified King and the Crown Prince fled from their palace and took refuge in the Russian Legation, where they remained for two years. There they were completely under the control of the astute minister, who became the *de facto* ruler of the country just as Yuan Shi Kwai and Inouye had, in their turns, previously been. He cared nothing for the internal reform of Korea; so far from that, the more chaotic her Government became, the more likely was she to be a helpless prey whenever Russia might think the time had come to grasp it, and that time would come with the completion of the Trans-Siberian railway. In the meantime, every step that could consolidate Russian influence was taken. Russian officers were appointed as instructors to the Korean army, financial officials to the control of the treasury, civil advisers to the other administrative departments, and commercial concessions, involving substantial territorial rights that afforded plausible excuses for placing Russian troops and colonists in northern Korea, were easily obtained.

Japan endeavoured to repair the terrible blunder she had made in entrusting her representation to one so unfitted as Miura by sending, in his place, Baron

Komura, who was as conspicuous for the possession of all the qualities that fitted him for a difficult diplomatic post as Miura was the reverse, who was, in later years, the negotiator of the Portsmouth Treaty, Ambassador to Great Britain and Minister for Foreign Affairs, but even his great abilities could achieve nothing. Numerous efforts were made to come to an understanding with Russia, both at St Petersburg and in Tokio, but while Russia was willing enough to sign any conventions, she showed by her actions that she had no intention of abiding by them one moment longer than it suited her to do so.

It was not in Korea alone that her activity was manifested. She had in 1895, with the help of France and Germany, compelled Japan to restore to China the Liao Tung peninsula and the fortress of Port Arthur. Within less than three years she induced China to cede to her, on a so-called lease, the southern part of the peninsula and the fortress, in cynical disregard of all the alleged reasons for depriving Japan of what had been legitimately won in war. She thus acquired a fortress that was believed, when in capable hands, to be impregnable, whose situation rendered it of immense strategic importance, which furnished what she had been so long desiring, an ice-free port for her fleet on the Pacific. It was notified to the world that the right of entrance to the harbour would henceforth be limited to the warships of Russia and China, the latter, since the Japan war, being a non-existing quantity, and it soon became evident that the acquisition of Port Arthur was only a stepping-stone to that of the three rich provinces of China which combine to form Manchuria. Russia obtained from China the right of carrying her trans-Siberian railway through Manchuria, both to Port Arthur and to Vladivostok, and of guarding the line by her own troops. As no limit was placed on the number of the latter, or on the extent of territory they were supposed to guard, Russian garrisons soon became conspicuous throughout the three provinces, and even the capital Mukden, the birth-place of the Imperial Manchus, was not exempt. The Boxer rising in 1900 gave the opportunity for the undisguised annexation of a large strip of land on the right bank of the river Amur, which till then had been the boundary of Siberia and northern Manchuria, and a further plausible opportunity, with the military strength to take advantage of it, was only awaited to extend this annexation to the whole territory.

With a fortified naval base at Vladivostok on the East of Korea, another even stronger at Port Arthur on the West, and all Manchuria on the North in Russian hands, the ultimate fate of Korea would be sealed. Russia could take possession of the whole peninsula whenever she wished and Japan would

then have on her sea borders, only a few miles from
her own shores, a greedy and unscrupulous Power
of overwhelming military strength.   Korea in the
Russian grasp more than realized to Japan all the
possibilities that the most advanced Unionists profess
to foresee in a hostile Ireland under Home Rule and
in active sympathy with a strong naval Power at
war with Great Britain.   Or to take another parallel,
equally applicable to ourselves, she regarded such
an eventuality as equally pregnant with danger to
her own national existence as we should the absorp-
tion of Belgium and Holland by the German Empire.
The completion of the trans-Siberian Railway enabled Russia to make large increases in her troops,
her Pacific fleet was reinforced by battleships of the
first class and the fortifications of Port Arthur and
Vladivostok were strengthened by every means that
military engineering could devise to render them
impregnable.

Japan on her side was not idle.   Through all
these years, she was steadily developing her material
and military resources and both advanced by leaps
and bounds.   She was gradually but surely moving
towards the time when she could calmly contemplate
the results of a conflict even with Russia.   But
France was Russia's ally and it was known that the
alliance was not confined to Europe.   Germany had
already shown that she would not be indisposed to

act with Russia in the Far East, and however ready Japan might be to face Russia single-handed, she could not risk a conflict in which Russia could rely on the active co-operation of one and at least the sympathy of another great military Power.   Her difficulty was solved when the Treaty of Alliance with Great Britain, signed in London on January 30, 1902, gave her the assurance that if the juncture arose, she would, in her turn, not be left to meet it alone.

Two more years of diplomatic negotiation followed without change in Russia's methods.   Her representative in Japan and her other agents in the East blundered much as the Chinese Minister had done ten years previously.   They did not underestimate Japanese patriotism, but they entirely misjudged the completeness of Japan's military preparations and took little pains to conceal the contempt they felt for her as an adversary on either sea or land. Acting on their information Russia thought she could continue to flout, with the same cynical effrontery as before and with absolute impunity to herself, every effort that was made by Japan to provide the safe-guards that were thought to be essential for the independence of Korea and her own territorial integrity.

Patience, no matter how long-suffering, has its limits, and those which Japan had prescribed for herself in this case were transgressed in 1904, and on the 10th of February war was formally declared in Tòkio. The date was one of great historical associations. It was one day earlier than that on which Jimmu, the first Emperor, ascended the throne more than 2,500 years before, and than that on which the reigning Emperor had promulgated, in 1889, the constitution to his people. It was two days earlier than that on which the Anglo-Japanese alliance was published to the world.

The command of the sea was essential to the accomplishment of Japan's plan of campaign. She had a powerful fleet in full commission under the supreme command of Admiral Togo, the officer who, as captain of the "Naniwa," struck the first blow in the war with China, but that of Russia was, on paper, somewhat stronger, and it could in time be reinforced from the Baltic, while Japan had neither reserves to fall back upon nor possible means, while the war lasted, of acquiring new ships of the first class to replace any that were lost. She could not therefore afford to stake everything on one general engagement, but her difficulty was solved by the enterprise of Togo and the supineness of the Russians in their avowed contempt for their enemy. The main Russian fleet was at anchor in the roadstead outside the harbour of Port Arthur, but four first-class cruisers were far away at Vladivostok and

one, with a gunboat, was at Chemulpo.   Not only
was no attempt made to unite these scattered ships,
but so little belief was felt in the possibility of Japan
venturing on war that the most ordinary precautions
were neglected by the fleet at Port Arthur.   On the
night of the 8th of February most of the officers
were actually on shore at a ball.   Those left on
board were probably thinking of nothing less than
a coming attack, when suddenly the Japanese
flotilla of torpedo boats swooped down and, at the
most trifling cost to themselves, inflicted such damage
on the Russian fleet that three of its most formidable
fighting units were incapacitated for further service.
On the following day, the two vessels at Chemulpo
were destroyed by an overwhelming force, after an
attempt at resistance in which, gallant as it was,
not a particle of damage was done either to the men
or the ships of the Japanese.   Both these events took
place before the formal declaration of war.   They
gave Japan the undisputed command of the sea, and
when the declaration was made she knew that she
could land her troops when and where she would.
Russia tried to redeem her first naval failure by
fitting out a great fleet in the Baltic, but when it
arrived in Japanese waters, manned with half-trained
crews and its ships foul after the long voyage round
the Cape, it was totally destroyed in one afternoon.
The battle was fought on May 28, 1905, near the

island of Tsushima, from which it takes its name, and it was in its results the most decisive and complete since Trafalgar.

Space permits us to devote but a few words to the campaign on land. There, too, victory attended the Japanese arms but it was gained at heavy cost. The great fortress of Port Arthur was once more taken after a siege which lasted six months, and six great battles were fought, one of which (Liao-Yang) lasted for nine and another (Mukden) for fourteen days. The end of all was a deadlock. The Russian armies, though repeatedly defeated, still presented a bold front and Japan was coming to the limit of her resources both of men and money. Then the President of the United States intervened and peace was established by the Treaty of Portsmouth (New Jersey, U.S.A.) which was signed on August 29, 1905.

The provisions of the treaty were in some degree a repetition of those of the treaty of Shimonoseki. Japan's preponderating influence in Korea, political, military and economic, was once more admitted. The southern extremity of the Liao Tung Peninsula and Port Arthur were once more ceded to her. Russia also undertook to evacuate Southern Manchuria, and as China had ceded Formosa so did Russia now cede the southern half of Saghalin. Japan also obtained control of the southern section of the Manchurian Railway for a length of 521 miles from the terminus

at Port Arthur together with all the collateral privileges that Russia had extorted from China. Those
were her fruits of the war, which had cost her
more than 170 millions sterling and 230,000 of her
soldiers, killed or wounded. No war indemnity
was paid and while Japan had secured in the fullest
degree the objects for which she had fought, she had
now to face all the burthens of what was, relative
to her resources, an enormous national debt and to
assume the obligation of safe-guarding her new
possessions and interests on the mainland of Asia.
Provision had to be made for the interest and
amortisation of the national debt, but this necessity
did not deter the Government from immediately
adopting measures to ensure the large increase in
the fighting strength of the nation that was demanded
by its new responsibilities.

Six divisions were added to the army, raising the
total from thirteen, the number before the Russian
War, to nineteen. Each division is in itself a complete fighting unit, comprising infantry, cavalry,
artillery, engineers and transport, and greater relative increases were made in the latter branches of
each division than in the infantry. Improvements
were effected in the arms, organisation and general
equipment of the whole army. The conscription
law was altered and the period of service with the
colours reduced from three to two years, but that

in the reserve was simultaneously extended from four to ten years, the results of the two measures being that it became possible to enrol annually a much larger number of conscripts than formerly, while the first reserve was increased from 200,000 to 500,000 men. The total strength of the army on its peace footing is now close upon 250,000 and it is estimated that, in little more than ten years, Japan will be able to put into the field for foreign service, should occasion require it, not less than 1,500,000 men, all fully trained soldiers, while another million men of the "reinforcing reserve" (Hoju), conscripts who, though physically fit, are not called to the colours and receive only a short training of a few months' duration spread over two years, will be available both for the defence of the country against invasion and also for filling up vacancies in the first fighting lines. Every man cheerfully undergoes all the sacrifices that are necessary to make him efficient and he is ready whenever called upon.

No less care was given to the extension of the navy than to the army. Before the Russian War Japan possessed, exclusive of torpedo boats, 79 war vessels with a total displacement of 274,000 tons, of which six were first-class battleships, the whole being manned by a personnel of 46,000 officers and men. Two battleships and eight cruisers were lost during the war, but five battleships and eleven cruisers were captured from the Russians. An extensive building programme was initiated after the war, the result of which is that the navy now consists of 124 ships with a displacement of over 500,000 tons, including 16 battleships and 13 armed cruisers of the first class, manned by a personnel of over 48,000 officers and men. Arsenals, dock-yards, powder factories and land fortifications were also increased in size and efficiency, and all the measures necessary for naval construction completed so as to render Japan absolutely independent in the construction and arming of ships of the largest size and most modern design.

These increases in the fighting strength required equally large increases in the national expenditure. The annual budget which, previous to the war, provided for an army expenditure of about five millions sterling and for the navy of less than three millions rose to eleven millions and eight millions respectively, and these charges added to the interest on the national debt, necessitated an immense increase in taxation. The national revenue before the war was twenty-six millions sterling. It is now nearly fifty-eight millions, the yield from taxation alone having been increased from fourteen to thirty-two millions sterling.

Industry and trade have developed and the

9—2

general economic conditions of the country improved to an extent that has enabled the people to bear the new financial burthens without distress, and though retrenchment has been one of the principal planks in the platform of the leading political parties, the Government has been able to maintain the foreign credit and policy of the nation unhampered by the dread of serious financial embarrassments at home. The Anglo-Japanese alliance was re-ratified and extended in 1905. An *entente* was established with Russia and France two years later and the bonds thus created were morally strengthened when the trend of European politics brought Great Britain into close association with the two latter Powers. Japan has been able to proceed on the path which she had marked out for herself in Korea without fear of further complications in the future, of which the possibility would never have been wholly wanting had Russia continued to adhere to her old policy of expansion southwards in the Far East and to cherish feelings of one day recovering by her arms all that she had lost in the war.

At the very outset of the war, when Japan had secured command of the sea but before the first land battle had been fought on the banks of the Yalu, a new treaty was concluded between Japan and Korea, by which the latter pledged herself to adopt

Marquis Inouye

the advice of the former in regard to the improvement
of the administration, while Japan in return undertook to secure both "the external and internal peace
and the independence and integrity of Korea," as
well as "the safety and repose of the Imperial House"
—the King had, in 1897, assumed the title of and
been recrowned as Emperor, an act which emphasized
his complete freedom from vassalage to China. A
supplement to this treaty, signed in 1905, gave to
Japan the control of Korea's foreign relations and
Prince Ito—he was advanced to the highest rank in
the peerage after the war, and Count Inouye was at
the same time advanced to the Marquisate—was
appointed Resident-General, and his great abilities
and experience were thenceforward devoted to the
task, which he had accomplished with such brilliant
success in his own country, of effecting the complete
political and social reform of Korea. His position
was, however, in some degree similar to that of
Marquis Inouye. He was still only an adviser, and
though the Korean Government had pledged itself to
accept his advice, when it failed to do so, as was
often the case, he had no means of enforcing the
measures he thought necessary. A strong step was
unavoidable. In July 1907, the Emperor was forced
to abdicate, after a reign of 40 years, in favour of his
son and simultaneously a new convention was signed,
which practically vested the Resident-General with

supreme legislative and executive authority.   He
was now no longer an adviser but an administrator
able to enforce his will, and a sweeping campaign of
reform was at once instituted, which affected not only
every branch of the Government, from the court to
the most remote local prefectures, but the whole
social system of the nation.

A great measure of success was achieved not only
in administrative and legislative reforms, but also in
the development of education, industry, sanitation and
communications, but Prince Ito was not fated to see
the results of his work.   On October 26, 1909, he was
assassinated by one of the people whom he was trying
to benefit, and his great career came to an end,
a career which, both in the service he rendered to
his country and in the world-wide reputation as a
statesman which it brought to him, is only paralleled
in modern times by those of Lincoln, Bismarck and
Cavour.   The pride in which his memory is held in
his own country may well be shared by Great Britain.
The short education which he received in his youth
in England and the knowledge that he then acquired
of the foundations of the political and commercial
greatness of the British Empire were the mainsprings
of all the great efforts of his manhood, by which he
transformed his own country from a puny and insignificant Asiatic despotism, torn by internecine
strife and fettered by the iron shackles of feudalism,

into one of the great constitutional, military and commercial Powers of the world.

With his death the last hopes faded of preserving even the nominal independence of Korea. The regime of a protectorate which, through him, Japan was endeavouring to render effective, threatened to collapse when the great guiding hand was taken away, and before another year had passed, on August 29, 1910, the last step was taken and Korea was formally annexed to the Japanese Empire. The step had been under consideration even before Ito's death, and it is possible that he may have seen its ultimate necessity as the only means of Japan attaining in its completest sense all she had fought for in her two great wars. She had persistently disclaimed any desire for territorial aggression. She had in her treaty of 1904 with Korea unequivocally pledged herself to secure the independence and integrity of the Korean Empire, and when she did so she honestly intended to observe her undertaking to its uttermost limits. But facts had proved too strong for her. All the sacrifices she had made—which included a very large direct outlay on Korea's behalf—had failed to furnish definite prospects of the effective regeneration of the unhappy, ill-governed kingdom, or of the permanent reform of glaring social abuses that had lasted for centuries. The only hope for the future lay in Japan openly assuming the full responsibility of the administration in name as well as in deed.

Her colony of Formosa has been successfully exploited and, by good government, order has been maintained and the great natural resources of the island so well used that it now promises to become a valuable commercial asset to the Empire. What has been achieved in Formosa will no doubt in due time be also achieved in Korea, when all the black records of the past have been erased from the memories of its people by the just and humane treatment which the Emperor ordered his officials to extend to them and by a security of life and property that they never knew when under their own authorities.

The long Korean chapter in the history of Japan's Foreign Relations is now closed and the main source of her external complications is gone. Neither Great Britain nor Russia, the two Powers most materially interested, raised one word of protest against the annexation. Great Britain was Japan's ally and the *entente* with Russia facilitated the specific delimitation of the future spheres of both in the Far East of the Asiatic continent. Russia has abandoned all her old projects of territorial expansion to the South, and Japan has acquired a free hand in South Manchuria, where she has opened for herself a path not unlike that which was the object of Russia before the war. The rights which she obtained by the treaty of Portsmouth, subsequently ratified by a convention with China, have not only been utilised to the fullest extent, but even attempts on the part of other nations to share in the development of railway construction, with its consequent commercial advantages in Manchuria, have been successfully resisted. Japanese troops are now in Southern Manchuria for the same ostensible purpose of guarding the existing railway lines as were formerly the Russian. Japanese immigrants have been flocking into and settling in the province, and though parliament has recently put its veto on the large increase of the army in Korea that the military authorities demanded as a necessary measure for the maintenance of Japan's interests, every present indication leads to the assumption that the control which is now exercised over Southern Manchuria is intended to be permanent and that continued political unrest in China may even afford plausible grounds for open annexation.

Since the war, Japan's only external controversies have been with the United States of America, the country on which, throughout the early years of the Imperial Government, she relied as her best political friend, the one in strongest sympathy with all her national aspirations. Her action in Manchuria has been one subject of these controversies, but their beginning is to be found in more domestic incidents.

Large numbers of Japanese traders, artisans and skilled agriculturists emigrated to the Pacific slope both of the United States and of Canada, attracted not only by the high wages that were obtainable for their very efficient labour, but also by the commercial and agricultural openings that could be profitably exploited by those who either brought a small capital with them or afterwards acquired it while in service. As small tradesmen, as skilled mechanics, and as fruit growers, living and carrying on their occupations at far less cost than was possible for their competitors of European descent, they were always able to under-sell the latter and acquired therefore a very consider-able degree of prosperity.

They were not welcome either in British Columbia or in California, but their numbers continued to increase through the facilities provided for them by large emigration companies in Japan, and the result was an outburst both in British Columbia and in California of anti-Asiatic prejudice, which, in 1907, attained to such dimensions that the local legislatures were forced to pass Immigration Acts generally restricting the further ingress of Asiatics, but in both cases mainly directed against Japanese.   The Californian legislature added insult to injury by debarring the children of Japanese, who were already resident in the State, from the privilege of attending the State schools.

These measures provoked intense indignation in
Japan and were a cause of great embarrassment to
the Governments of Canada and the United States.
Under the treaties, Japanese had clearly the right of
entering and residing in the territories of both without limitation of any kind as to occupations or
districts, and an obligation lay on the Governments
to see that the provisions of the treaties were not
violated by individual State legislatures which, whatever was the extent of the local autonomy enjoyed
by them, were subordinate to the central Governments in all Imperial affairs.   A serious international
difficulty was threatened, but it was happily averted
by the good sense and conciliatory disposition of the
Government of Japan.   No abatement was made of
the admitted treaty rights, but in Japan restrictions
were placed on emigration which were effective in
limiting that across the Pacific to a very moderate
scale and in confining the emigrants to persons who
were not likely to become industrial competitors with
Europeans.   This question was thus settled, for the
time being, but it has, at the time of writing, apparently been revived in California in a somewhat
acute form, one which, if it continues, must cause
serious friction between the two Governments.   That
of the United States cannot, under the constitution,
interfere with the sovereign autonomy which each individual State enjoys in its local affairs.   That of Japan is

in no mood to brook any infraction of its treaty rights or any derogatory discrimination against its people.

Their growing trans-Pacific trade caused the United States to give increased attention to affairs in China and to lend their diplomatic support to the preservation both of China's territorial integrity and of the principle of the "open door," by which all nations enjoy equal commercial opportunities throughout the whole Empire. Japan's actions in Manchuria, with their possible eventualities, were not unnoticed in the States. An effort was made in 1910 to counteract them in the proposal of the Secretary of State (Mr Knox) that all the railways in Manchuria should be neutralised, but its only direct result was the conclusion of a further agreement between Japan and Russia for the defence of their mutual interests and the maintenance of the *status quo*. The rebuff has not diminished the active interest of the United States in the future of China, which in her turn, under her new republican Government, evinces a growing desire to rely on the United States for both political and financial support. The mutual attitudes of the United States and Japan across the Pacific are now not unlike those of the German Empire and Great Britain in Europe, outwardly friendly but with a strong undercurrent of mistrust in the militant sections of both nations. Both are aspirants for the hegemony of the Pacific.

The controversies between the United States and Japan gave rise to serious apprehension in Great Britain as to the obligations of the alliance in the event of a war between the two Powers and the complications which might arise under the General Treaty of Arbitration, then being negotiated with the United States, on the one side and the Treaty of Alliance with Japan on the other. A new Treaty of Alliance, to continue in force for ten years, was therefore concluded in 1911, by which modifications, intended to remove this apprehension, were introduced into the old, and in the same year a new commercial treaty was also negotiated and signed, the latter containing a special tariff clause under which the customs dues are fixed on the principal British imports to Japan. These had been so largely increased by the Japanese legislature in 1910 as to threaten a very serious diminution of British trade, and a commercial was therefore superimposed on the political grievance created by the Alliance. The former, if not removed in its absolute entirety, was so materially softened by the new treaty as to leave no reasonable ground for discontent on the part of the manufacturer in Great Britain. The customs dues now levied in Japan are much heavier than they were, but the aggregate value of British imports has substantially increased, and by the Alliance Great Britain is, at a time when it is advisable for her to concentrate her whole naval strength in home waters, freed from the obligation of maintaining a strong fleet in the Far East. Great Britain can pride herself in the knowledge that her example originally fired the ambition of Japan. She has her material reward in being able to count upon the faithful support of an ally, whose own military strength and natural advantages constitute an impregnable defence against all the world.

CHAPTER X

THE EMPEROR MEIJI

THE Emperor Mutsu Hito (Gentle Pity) died on the 30th of July 1912, and, in accordance with immemorial custom, with him died the personal name that he had borne in life. He will be known in history by his posthumous title, the Emperor Meiji (Enlightened Government), the year name so happily chosen at the beginning of his reign and since amply vindicated in all the great administrative changes that have combined to render the name eminently applicable to the reign. In taking the year name as the posthumous title of the Emperor, a new departure was made, but it is possible that the precedent thus created will be followed in future ages. The posthumous titles of all the former Emperors were founded on the quality that most favourably characterised the holder in his lifetime, such as "Divine Valour," "Honour the Gods," "Modesty" (in the case of an Empress), "Pious Enlightenment," or were taken from a locality in or in the neighbourhood of Kioto with which the Emperor had some personal connection. Year periods were formerly never synchronous with reigns. New ones were not begun at the beginning of a reign but more or less frequently during its continuation. The late Emperor's father, for example, ascended the throne in the third year of Kokwa (great transformation), and three years passed before a new period was begun, while, though his whole reign only lasted for twenty years, it comprised no less than seven year periods. The period of Meiji began in the second calendar year of the late reign and continued unchanged till its close, and there was therefore a reason for giving its title to the Emperor that did not exist in the case of any of his predecessors. Apart from that, no previous sovereign of Japan ever merited, in his personal character or in his government, the title chosen to honour his memory more than did he to whom that of Meiji has been given.

The Emperor Meiji was the 121st member of the dynasty which, in an unbroken line of succession, claims to have occupied the throne of Japan since the Emperor Jimmu first ascended it in the year 660 B.C. Modern research has reduced to pure mythology the first ten centuries of the so-called history of Japan, and it is only from the sixth century of the Christian era that the national annals are such as to bear the light of scientific criticism. Thenceforward they may justly be called authentic history and, however visionary may be the claim of the Imperial House of Japan to the more ancient descent, there is no doubt that from the sixth century it has consecutively occupied the throne, and it is therefore, beyond all cavil, the oldest reigning family in the world. Imperial rescripts emphasize the duration and immutability of the dynasty : "We, sitting on the throne that has been occupied by our Imperial ancestors for 2,500 years" : "The throne of our ancestors of a lineal succession unbroken for ages eternal" : "We, by the grace of Heaven, seated on a throne occupied by the same dynasty from time immemorial," are the ordinary opening words of important rescripts, and they are reverentially accepted by the Emperor's subjects with the same unquestioning faith that devout and orthodox Christians tender to the most sacred utterances in Holy Writ.

No other Sovereign or Pontiff on earth occupies the same position as the Emperor of Japan. In the eyes of his subjects he is the vicegerent on earth of the gods in Heaven, vested with their divine attributes of love, benevolence and all-seeing wisdom. In his earthly functions he is both sovereign and pope, who reigns equally in the love and veneration of his people. All the achievements of his statesmen and generals are believed to be due to the virtues which he has inherited from his ancestors and which, in his lifetime, he practises as the Father of his people. It was no spirit of empty flattery that prompted Oyama and Togo, the respective commanders-in-chief of all the military and naval forces in the Russian War, to ascribe to him all the merit of their great victories nor Ito that of his domestic and foreign statesmanship. They only voiced, in doing so, the faith that was deeply implanted in their own hearts and in those of all their fellow-subjects and was the foundation of the fervent loyalty that rendered death for his sake a glorious martyrdom.

The birth of the Emperor Meiji has been already mentioned in this volume. His early years were passed in the well-guarded seclusion of the Court at Kioto, but when he was little beyond the threshold of his boyhood he had direct experience of the civil war that preceded the Restoration. The Imperial palace was guarded by the forces of the Shogunate, and Choshiu, who had thrown down the gauntlet of rebellion, determined to drive them from their post, and to obtain direct access to the Emperor and his countenance of the revolt against the Shogun. For a whole day and night the battle continued around the palace with varying fortunes; the gates were

taken and retaken, bullets fell thickly within the
precincts of the palace, many reaching the innermost
Impérial apartments, and the din of musketry and
artillery was incessant. Choshiu was defeated and
the palace was saved, but the city, "surrounded by
a ninefold circle of flowers" (flames), was destroyed,
and "nothing was left of it but a burnt and scorched
desert."

Before this battle the Emperor had already, when
he reached the eighth year of his age, been declared
to be the heir-apparent to the throne, and in his
fifteenth year he succeeded his father. It cannot
be supposed that, at that tender age, he can have
exercised a direct influence on the early political
events of his reign, but it would-have been within
his capacity to have withheld his sanction from the
ministers who were subverting the most sacred traditions of the Empire, and inflicting what his father
would have considered the most degrading humiliations on the Imperial dignity when they declared, in
his name, that foreign friendship should be cultivated
and the Court opened to the diplomatic representatives of Foreign Powers. Fortunately, he had had
the benefit of tutors more enlightened and liberal-
minded than the majority of the courtiers, and the
results of their teaching were sufficient to counteract
the reactionary sentiments that might have been
imbibed from his bigoted father. The germs of the

good sense and sound judgment, which he displayed
in manhood, must, however, have been active while
he was still a boy, and without those qualities it is
not likely that any tutors, no matter how capable
or how secure in the affections of their pupil, could
so speedily have overcome all the prejudices that
were founded on filial love and respect, the strongest
of all obligations in the Japanese code of morality.
It has been already told that the first Europeans
admitted to his presence were impressed by his tact
and readiness. It is not an extravagant supposition
that his own ministers may have had equal reason to
appreciate and benefit by the more sober qualities
which enabled him to be in full sympathy with their
reforms.

The historians of those days relate no instance
in which the ministers found him an obstacle to
their measures. He received the hitherto hated and
despised foreigners without demur. When he was
advised that the future government of his Empire
might be facilitated by the transfer of his residence
from Kioto to Yedo, he left the home of his childhood and youth, and of all his ancestors for more
than a thousand years, and, resisting the entreaties
of devoted disciples of the old school who implored
him not to forsake the venerable city that was
hallowed by so many sacred memories, he uncom-
plainingly made a new home in the mushroom capital

of the Shoguns, the seat of their government which had usurped all the prerogatives of his Imperial fore-fathers. And when he was further advised that he should no longer be a hidden mystery to his people, though remembering how his own father in his lifetime had been shrouded from them, he freely and unostentatiously showed himself in public, driving about the streets of Tokio, with a small escort, without disturbing the daily avocations of the citizens, and taking part in functions and ceremonies where he could be seen by all who cared to look upon him.

How great this change was may be easily estimated from the description already given of his first journey to Osaka, and from that of his first journey to Tokio. In was in October 1868 that he left Kioto for his new capital, 300 miles away. He was 28 days on the road, carried in a palanquin in which he was screened from all onlookers, and on both sides of which double lines of courtiers, all in the stately silken robes of old Japan, walked in slow and solemn step. An escort of 2,000 courtiers and guards attended him throughout the entire route. All bystanders fell upon their knees as his procession approached and, as he passed, remained with heads bent reverentially to the ground and in profound silence that was only broken by the triple clapping of the hands that prefaces all Japanese prayers. No one dared to lift the eye even to the

level of the palanquin that bore him. "All seemed
to hold their breaths for very awe as the mysterious
Presence, on whom few are privileged to look and
live, was passing slowly by."

Early in the following year he returned to Kioto
to celebrate the third anniversary of his father's death
(a sacred duty marking the close of the period of deep
mourning that has to be performed by Japanese sons
of all classes in life) and his own marriage, which took
place on March 9, 1869. The lady chosen to share
his throne was Haruko, a daughter of the Ichijo
branch of the Fujiwara family. The origin of this
family, like that of the Imperial House, is shrouded
in myth, but an unimpeachable lineage can be traced
back to the 7th century. Six hundred years later
the family was divided into five branches, of which
the Ichijo was one. All of these still exist, their
respective heads holding the highest rank in the
modern peerage. The marriage, although childless,
proved eminently fortunate. The Empress did not
begin to take part in public functions so early as her
husband. The old traditions that had to be overcome in her case were even more severe than in his,
but from the time she did so, she played a true
woman's part in all works of charity, and above all
in the promotion of female education and in raising
the general social conditions of her countrywomen.
Women, prior to the Restoration, except in the

lower agricultural and trading classes, had no other functions than to be the humble and uncomplaining servitors of their husbands and the mothers of their children. They enjoyed more freedom than in other Oriental countries, but they were taught from infancy that their lot in life was obedience, to their fathers while maidens, to their husbands while wives, and to their eldest sons while widows, and no education fitted them to become the intellectual companions of men. It is mainly to the Empress that they owe the emancipation from these conditions which is one of the most marked features in the modern life of Japan.

After his marriage the Emperor returned to Tokio where he was soon followed by his bride. There both afterwards lived continuously till they were parted by death. Both occasionally visited other parts of the Empire, and the Emperor made many state progresses through all parts of his dominions, but Tokio was always their home, and neither showed any inclination to leave it, even to seek temporary refuge from its oppressive heat in summer or from its bitter winter cold. Their presence did much to restore the prosperity of the city under the Tokugawas, when in wealth, population, industry and intelligence it was by far the foremost in the Empire. When the Tokugawas fell, Yedo fell with them, and for a time it seemed as if all its former glory was gone for ever.

But Tokio sprang from its ruins, and, before many years had passed, had not only regained but far surpassed the most imposing acme of the old prosperity.

To compare Tokio of the present day with Yedo as it was, even when the present writer first knew it little more than forty years ago, when the Tokugawas had just surrendered their sceptre, would be like comparing London of the days of Charles II with London as we now daily see it. Yedo was a lovely city, one in which it was a joy to live, with its spacious parks and temple gardens, its great orchards, even in its very heart, of cherry, plum and pear trees, each in turn bright with their masses of fragrant blossom ; its stately palaces of the daimio, with their massive gateways and granite bastions ; and its streets, with never a sound to break the rigid decorum of their silence, thronged with silk-clad, sword-girded samurai, on foot or on horseback, but in either case proceeding gravely and solemnly as became their rank and dignity. The masses of the people, if serfs, were contented and happy and not a trace of squalid poverty was to be seen even in the poorest quarters. But the city had another aspect. It was equally wanting in sanitation and police. At night it was in its outward appearance a vast solitude, shrouded in Cimmerian darkness, and if there were no foot-pads to be dreaded by the few belated wayfarers, drunken samurai returning from wild orgies in brothels or taverns, ready to use their terrible swords, with or without provocation, either on their humble fellow-countrymen or on any European who was unfortunate enough to cross their path, or in brawls, that were only ended by death, with others of their own rank, were a terror from which peaceful citizens were never free. The samurai in his dignity, in the day-time, was as stately and picturesque as a courtier of Louis XIV. At night, the dissolute members of the same class, of whom there were many, were as quarrelsome and dangerous as the clansmen in the streets of Edinburgh at the beginning of the 18th century.

Tokio of the present day has all the amenities of the London of George V. It is a more comfortable, convenient, safe and healthy place in which to live, but all that made Yedo so picturesque has gone. Only one feature of its medieval and feudal splendour has been preserved. The deep moats, massive walls and turf-clad glacis that encircled the palace of the Shogun still surround the palace of the Emperor and have lost none of their old grandeur. The pine and cherry trees still line the moat edges and the walls, and myriads of water fowl still find a sanctuary in the moats. Everything else is gone. Even the parks have been disfigured by architectural monstrosities in glaringly-red bricks, and the son of the stately silk-robed samurai now hurries, in a tweed suit and a felt hat, to his desk in a bank in a noisy, crowded, electric tram-car. At night the main streets are as brilliant, populous, noisy and safe as Piccadilly; they are entirely exempt from Piccadilly's plague spot in that there is no open display of female vice, and the danger that confronts the peaceful pedestrian is no longer the sword of the samurai but the motor of the road-hog.

It is difficult for a foreigner to attempt to estimate the direct share which the Emperor had in all the marvellous progress of his Empire. No sovereign in the history of the world has ever been better served in every department of his government, whether military or civil. None has ever commanded so devoted a people. But that the Emperor was well served was largely owing to himself. He possessed, in an eminent degree, what is perhaps the most precious attribute of a sovereign, the faculty of judging men, of selecting the best among them as his advisers, and he gave to those whom he selected his complete confidence and a support that never wavered in its loyalty. It is known that he was not only industrious, but industrious even to a degree that would not misbecome a man who had to make his name and earn his livelihood in an arduous profession. He presided in person at important meetings of his cabinet, when vital affairs of state had to be discussed and decided, and read not only the official reports of his ministers and the minutes of his parliaments, but the leading journals in the press. He had occasionally to decide between conflicting views of those whom he most trusted, and did so with firmness that brooked no contradiction, and without reservation of any kind. When only 21 years of age, as has been already told, he prevented war with Korea, though nearly the whole nation demanded it, and by his decision he had to sacrifice the future services of some of those who had done much to establish him on his throne. Twenty years later, it was he again who decided that Japan must accept the humiliation of yielding to the three Powers, and it was only his decision that reconciled the nation to the sacrifice of what had been fairly won in war. When a refractory parliament rejected the naval estimates that were considered essential for the national safety, he publicly declared that the parliament must give way and it did, awed into prompt submission and shamed perhaps by his sacrifice of a substantial portion of his own civil list. Many other incidents might be quoted, and it may be assumed that the firmness he showed in great was not wanting in less important affairs and that at no period of his reign did he ever permit himself to fall into the rôle of a dummy ruler.

His interest in both his army and navy was manifested by his presence at all manœuvres and reviews that were held on a large scale. No inclemency of weather ever deterred him, and he was equally assiduous in the performance of the more ornamental functions of a sovereign. Hospitals were visited, railways, docks and other great public undertakings were opened by him in person, and even jails knew his presence. No work of public benefit, charity or mercy ever sought his personal interest in vain, and his private purse was always open for the relief of the national distress that ensued on fire, earthquake, flood or pestilence, calamities from which his country suffered often and heavily. The rapidity and extent of the purely material advance of Japan, military, industrial and commercial, has thrown into the shade the progress she has made in the domain of science. She may be said to have been absolutely ignorant of even the elements of Western science prior to the Restoration. Now there are few branches in which her sons, if they have not won distinction beyond their own borders, have not, at least, proved themselves capable experts, fully competent both to practise and to teach. That this is so is due to the encouragement which the Emperor gave to higher education in Japan and to the continuation in Europe of the studies of the best pupils of the home universities.

He had only two amusements, horse riding and the composition of poetry. He rode both boldly and

well, better than most of his subjects who have not
had a special training. Verse-making is a necessary
accomplishment of every educated Japanese gentle-
man and not an uncommon one among women. It
holds the place that Latin versification did in England
in the days of Addison. The beauties of nature—
beauties such as trees bending beneath a weight of
snow or an autumn moon reflected in a placid lake,
to which the English sense is often blind but which
appeal strongly to the Japanese—and the vicissitudes
of human life are its chief themes. In this art the
Emperor excelled. Many of his poems have been
published and they confirm the estimate of his
character that is founded on his public actions,
breathing as they do the most tender sentiments
of compassion and pity. He had his own full share
of human sorrow. The Empress was childless but
fourteen children were born to him from the four
ladies who were united to him as Jugo. Nine died
in infancy or childhood, leaving one son, who is now
the Emperor, and four daughters who have grown to
womanhood. Two of his nearest relatives sacrificed
their lives in the China war, and of the devoted ministers and generals who served him at the Restoration,
to all of whom he was attached by ties of gratitude
and affection, only five survived him.

His reign was the longest in the authentic history
of Japan. It lasted 45 years, and its end came with

grief and sorrow to all his people. His active life
was spent in Tokio, where he died in his modern
palace, but his last resting place is in a mausoleum
at Kioto, built in the old style of Japan, amid the
solemn and silent groves where rest also the remains
of his ancestors during more than a thousand years.
With his death ended the period of Meiji, during
which the evolution of New Japan was begun and
carried to its end. In all the history of the civilisation of the world there is nothing that can compare
with its rapidity and completeness.

NOTES

In 1897 Japan adopted a gold standard of currency, the unit
being the yen, the sterling equivalent of which is 2s. 0½d. Prior to
1897, the yen was a silver coin, the sterling value of which fluctuated
in ratio with the market price of silver. Silver was a steadily
depreciating commodity and the sterling value of the yen gradually
fell from about 4s. 2d. in 1874 to less than half that amount in 1894.
Allowance must be made for this fall in estimating in sterling the
progress of the foreign trade of Japan which is described on page 92,
but the yen has been retained in the text as the only available common
denominator. The value of the Chinese tael, a silver token, else-
where mentioned, at the close of the Japan-China war was roughly
about 3s.

"Hara-kiri,"—literally "belly-cut"—suicide by disembowelling,
was the prerogative of the Samurai class. It was instituted in the
middle ages in order that Samurai who had committed crimes
which, though meriting the punishment of death, were not in themselves disgraceful, should by putting an end to their own lives escape
the indignity of dying by the hands of the common executioner. In

these cases, it was carried out in the presence of witnesses, with much formality, in accordance with a very rigid code of etiquette, on the command either of the Government or of the suicide's superiors in his own Fief. Death in this way involved no degradation either to the sufferer or his family. In time, it came to be committed voluntarily, either when a Samurai had, for any reason, lost all interest in life, or when (by far the more common cause) he desired to make the strongest protest that was in his power against some act, conduct, or policy of his superiors. Every Samurai carried two swords, a long and a short one. The first was to be used against enemies, the second on himself. He never parted from either. When abroad, they were both worn in his girdle; when indoors, both lay close beside him, whether by day or night, and he was trained from his infancy to be ready to use either for its specific purpose at a moment's notice. When the act was performed by command, the short sword was thrust into the belly by the suicide, but he was then immediately decapitated by a "Second," who stood beside him with drawn sword, and who was generally either a relative or a close friend. The physical agony was, therefore, momentary. But, in voluntary cases, there was no ''Second'' and the belly was cut completely open by the suicide himself, so that the act was prolonged and excruciatingly painful. A full description of it is given in Lord Redesdale's *Tales of old Japan*, Lord Redesdale having himself witnessed the completion of a judicial sentence of this nature. Women of the Samurai class imitated their husbands, but in their case the throat and not the belly was cut. The last instances were the suicides of General Nogi and his wife on the death of the late Emperor.

Considerations of space have necessitated the omission of the Kurile Islands from the map of the Japanese Empire. These Islands, called by the Japanese "Chi-shima" or "the thousand isles" are 31 in number, and extend in a continuous chain from the north-east of Hokkaido to Cape Lopatka, the southern extremity of Kamchatka.

POSTSCRIPT

BOOKS ON JAPAN

The task heralded in the Introduction is now completed. The prescribed limits of space have confined it to a skeleton outline, but none of the great events of a great reign have been omitted and what has been told is, it is hoped, sufficient to enable the reader to form a logical conception of the forces which gave rise to the evolution of new Japan and of their results.

Some readers may desire to pursue the subject, and if they do, there is the most abundant material for their purpose. Books dealing with Japan, from every conceivable point of view, can be numbered by thousands and both their number and variety are sufficient to bewilder the seeker for knowledge, who has no expert guide to direct him in his choice. To such a one, we venture to submit the following, all of which are easy to read and are written by recognised authorities.

1. "Tales of Old Japan." 2 vols. Lord Redesdale. Tales, direct from Japanese sources, vividly illustrating life in the good old days of feudalism, told in the most graceful English. London, 1871.

2. "The Capital of the Tycoon." 2 vols. Sir Rutherford Alcock. A picturesque description of Japan and of life in Yedo, during the closing years of the Shogunate. London, 1863.

3. "Unbeaten Tracks in Japan." 2 vols. Miss Bird. Fourth edition. London, 1885.

4. "East and West." Sir E. Arnold. This and Miss Bird's are the two best of the many hundreds of books that have been written by travellers. London, 1896.

5. "Classical Poetry of the Japanese." Chamberlain. London, 1880.

6. "A History of Japanese Literature." Aston. London, 1897.

7. "Shinto. The Way of the Gods." Aston. An esoteric exposition of the indigenous religion of Japan, appealing only to the serious student. This and the two preceding works are the best in their respective subjects. London, 1905.

8. "Things Japanese." Chamberlain. An encyclopedia of information on a vast variety of interesting topics, arranged in alphabetical order. Fourth edition. London, 1902.

9. "The Mikado's Empire." Griffis. New York, 1876.

10. "Japan." Story of the Nations series. Murray. This and the preceding are histories from the earliest times, by American authors, the first also containing a description of the author's personal experiences in Japan. London, 1904.

11. "Japan and China." 12 vols. Brinkley. The author was one of the greatest of English scholars, a profound expert on every subject connected with Japan, and the work is worthy of his reputation. London, 1903–4.

12. "Japan." Encyclopædia Britannica. By the same author, equally worthy of his reputation and sufficiently comprehensive to satisfy those who have neither time nor opportunity to read his larger work. Eleventh edition. London, 1911.

13. "Europe and the Far East." Douglas. Describes the modern history, and especially the relations with China. Cambridge, 1913.

14. Lafcadio Hearn. All his works. A graceful writer, a keen observer, a philosophic critic, who loved Japan and knew as no other European has ever done its inner life to the core.

A score of other books might be named, on art, industry, travel, life, history, etc., both of old and recent date, but this list will probably be sufficient. The reception given by reviewers and the public to previous works by the present author tempts him, even at the risk it involves, to add their names, "The Story of Òld Japan," "The Story of Korea," and "Japan of the Japanese." In the two first named, he endeavoured to tell the histories of the two countries, which are as closely interwoven as those of England and France, in a style that rendered their perusal no greater task than that of an ordinary novel, and in the third he describes the social and economic progress of Modern Japan. The dates of publication of " Japan " in the Story of the Nations series and of " Europe and the Far East " are those of the latest editions, both of which contain additional chapters, also by the present author.

INDEX

L.

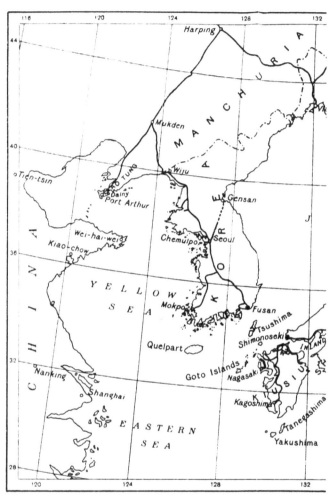

MAP OF JAPANESE
———— Railwa

:SE EMPIRE
ailways